HOW TO 'MEAT'
A BLONDE,
BRUNETTE OR REDHEAD

A Dating &
Cooking Guide

ORDERING INFORMATION

Order from **www.anotherblondemoment.com**
or **http://www.anotherblondemoment.com/**

For ordering your copy(ies) of **How to 'Meat' a Blonde, Brunette, or Redhead**, by mail please send $19.95 plus $6.00 Postage and Handling (Mississippi residents add 7% sales tax of $1.40) for **EACH** copy. Make checks payable to Another Blonde Moment, P. O. Box 320747, Flowood, MS 39232. Include name, address, city/state/zip, and phone number. Visa or MasterCard credit cards accepted. Must provide credit card number and expiration date. *Please note if you would like your book(s) signed to anyone particular.*

● ● ●

First Printing – July 2007

Copyright © 2007

ISBN Number: 0-9744972-2-3

Library of Congress Control Number: 2007905313

Printed in the United States of America
TOOF COOKBOOK DIVISION

Print smarter.
670 South Cooper Street
Memphis, TN 38104

BLONDICATION

This cookbook is blondicated to my children, Chelsea and Dakota. Both of you have been my inspiration since the beginning of Another Blonde Moment. To my husband, Terry, thank you for trying all my blonde recipes and cleaning up our 'blonde kitchen.' Also, thank you for putting me out when I was on fire, not getting too angry when I fell through the sheetrock and came through the ceiling, for not getting too mad when the candle broke my nose, and for taking care of me when I broke my foot.

To my best friend, Peggy, who has loved me in spite of me being me for 23 years.

To my Father, who helps me with the blonde dirty dishes and the many trips to the grocery store.

To my Mother, who has encouraged me each step of the way when I was cooking, packing, shipping or just thinking. My Mother would call and the first thing she would ask was, "Are you concentrating?" She knew if I was concentrating I couldn't talk to her.

Chip, Christy, Rachel, McKenzie, and Regan have taught me to forgive and directed me towards a more meaningful way of life.

Danna & Heath ate my cooking and tolerated my 'B.E.D. episode' while I was having my temporary melt-down.

Angel & Kevin gave me emotional and physical guidance. Mark & Lisa always entertained me.

Without these people in my life, this cookbook would not have been as enjoyable to do because each one of these people has provided a great deal of happiness to me.

Debbie Thornton

ABOUT THE AUTHORS

Co-author, Debbie Thornton, of the best selling cookbooks **ANY BLONDE CAN COOK: 269 WAYS TO A MAN'S HEART** and **ANY BLONDE CAN DO IT! A-Z** is a blonde A.D.D. cook. **Debbie** co-founded **Another Blonde Moment** less than 4 years ago, and has quickly blonded over 1,800 stores in 46 states with blonde merchandise.

Debbie Thornton

Debbie has cooked for over 150 local TV morning shows and prepared easy blonde recipes for all her audiences. She also travels around the United States giving knowledge and encouragement to women who want to start their own companies.

Chelsea Moore, (Debbie's brunette daughter), is a sophomore at The University of Mississippi, where she is a Marketing major.

Chelsea has always enjoyed creative writing, painting and fishing. She loves helping her Mom in the kitchen preparing meals for her family, friends, and neighbors.

Chelsea Moore

www.anotherblondemoment.com

4

How to **'STALK'** a Mate
RECIPES for 'FLIRTING'

'Mate Selection Soup'

5	gallons of self-confidence
1	appropriate flirting locale
1	nice, but flirty outfit
2	eyebrow-flashes
1	pair of eye gazes
2-3	constant smile exchanges
2	cups of posture

TAKE all your confidence with you.
PLACE yourself at the grocery store, sporting event, restaurant, a party or a learning place.
POUR flirty outfit into above location.
SET stove on **'HI'.**
HOLD eyebrow-flashes for more than 5 seconds.
MIX a 5 second eye gaze with a smile.
PROLONGED eye contact brings intense emotion.
FLIP hair side to side. **ADD** repeated leg crossing.
YIELDS: 1 cute couple.

It takes between 90 seconds & 4 minutes to decide if you are interested in someone.

• 55% is through body language
• 38% is the tone & speed of your voice
• 7% is through what you say

www.anotherblondemoment.com

RECIPES for 'FLIRTING'

'Anna Nicole Salad'

3	interpersonal zones
3	awareness of 'non-verbal leakage'
4	varieties of positive gestures
1	slight touch of the arm
4	cups of vocal signals
3	reciprocity conversations
1	prop for conversation
1	exchange of phone numbers

DECIDE which zone you need to be in.
'Social Zone' (12 to 4 feet)
'Personal Zone' (4 feet to 18 inches)
'Intimate Zone' (6 inches to 2 feet)
BE AWARE when it isn't working.
'Body Turn' (head toward you, body pointed away)
'Boredom Signs' (leaning backwards supporting head on 1 hand)
'Closed Posture' (arms folded, legs tightly crossed)
ADD 4 positive gestures.
SHIFT hands or head slightly when ending sentences.
USE downward hand gestures to emphasis a point.
OPEN-PALM hand movement projects attention.
RESPONSIVE MOVEMENT such as **nodding**, **throwing up your hands in surprise** or a **silent clap**.
TOUCHING adds a higher degree of intimacy.
USE tone, pitch, volume & speed of speech.
GIVE & Take, Share, Exchange with both parties talking & listening equally.
ADD fun sunglasses or talking stuffed animals.
EXCHANGE phone numbers, to top it off.

www.anotherblondemoment.com

Wild Game Recipes
(Dove, Duck, Venison)

How to 'STALK' a Mate
(RECIPES for 'FLIRTING')

www.anotherblondemoment.com

Wild Game Recipes
(Dove, Duck, Venison)

www.anotherblondemoment.com

Dove Artichoke Dip
"Doving to Choke"

2	**(14 ounce) cans artichoke hearts, drained, chopped**
2	**cups dove meat, chopped**
1	**cup mayonnaise**
1	**cup grated Parmesan cheese**
¼	**teaspoon garlic powder**
1	**teaspoon onion flakes**
1	**teaspoon cayenne pepper**
1	**teaspoon parsley flakes**
1	**teaspoon Cavendar's Greek seasoning**

COMBINE all ingredients in a bowl.
POUR in a pam-sprayed 9x13 baking dish.
BAKE at 350 degrees for 20-25 minutes.
SERVE with crackers.

FROM THE EDGE

Postcard from a blonde: Having a wonderful time. Where am I?

---

www.anotherblondemoment.com

Dove Wined
"Trochessett is Wining & Dining"

2	cups flour
1	Tablespoon salt
1	Tablespoon pepper
12	doves
$\frac{1}{2}$	cup oil
$\frac{1}{2}$	cup water
1	can cream of mushroom soup
1	celery stalk, chopped
$\frac{1}{2}$	cup red wine

COMBINE 1st 3 ingredients in a large bowl.
COAT doves in flour mixture.
BROWN dove in oil in a large skillet. **DRAIN**.
MIX last 4 ingredients in a bowl.
PLACE dove in a pam-sprayed 9x13 baking dish.
POUR wine mixture over dove. **COVER**.
BAKE at 350 degrees for 45 minutes.
SERVE on serving platter with bread.

www.anotherblondemoment.com

Duck Spread
"Chipper is Quacked"

3	ducks breasts
2	bay leaves
	Black pepper, to taste
	Salt, to taste
6	cups water
2	cups mayonnaise
1	celery stalk, chopped
1	teaspoon chili powder
2	hard-boiled eggs, chopped

COMBINE 1st 5 ingredients in a large pot.
BOIL until ducks are tender.
REMOVE ducks. **DEBONE**. **CHOP**.
COMBINE duck with last 4 ingredients.
MIX well. **SERVE** with crackers or on bread.

TOO MUCH SUGAR!

A nurse received a call from an anxious patient.
"I'm diabetic and I'm afraid I had too much sugar today."
"Are you light headed?" the nurse replied.
"NO!!!!", "I'm brunette."

---

www.anotherblondemoment.com

Venison Sausage Balls
"Stalked & Balled"

2	cups Bisquick
1/2	stick margarine, melted
1	egg, beaten
	Pepper, to taste
2	pounds ground venison sausage
4	cups shredded cheddar cheese

COMBINE all ingredients in a large bowl.
MIX well.
SHAPE in 1-inch balls.
PLACE on a cookie sheet.
BAKE at 350 degrees for 20 minutes.
ROLL balls around at least 2 times while baking.

Q: Why did the brunette throw water on her computer?
A: To surf the internet.

---

www.anotherblondemoment.com

Venison Sausage Slices
"Sliced for the Bailey's"

½	pound ground venison sausage, cooked, drained
⅓	cup Mozzarella cheese
½	cup sour cream
3	Tablespoons mayonnaise
2	Tablespoons green onions, chopped
½	teaspoon Worcestershire
1	teaspoon Blonde all-purpose seasoning
1	teaspoon Cavendar's Greek seasoning
10	bread slices, cut off crust, cut into 3 slices

COMBINE 1st 8 ingredients in a bowl.
PLACE bread slices on a cookie sheet.
SPOON venison mixture on bread slices.
BROIL until cheese melts.
SERVE hot.

www.anotherblondemoment.com

Duck Soup
"Danna Quacked Heath"

3	duck breasts, boiled, drained, chopped
1	can cream of celery soup
2	cans cream of mushroom soup
$\frac{1}{2}$	teaspoon salt
$\frac{1}{2}$	teaspoon pepper
$1\frac{1}{2}$	cups milk

COMBINE all ingredients in a large pot.
BRING to a boil. **LOWER** heat.
SIMMER for 1 hour, **covered**.
STIR occasionally.
SERVE over rice.

Q: What do you call a brunette in a room full of blondes?
A: Invisible.

---

www.anotherblondemoment.com

Venison Sausage Gumbo
"Mark it Dear"

1	package Creole gumbo mix
2	pounds venison link sausage, ¼ inch
8	cups water
1	onion, chopped
1	(16 ounce) bag whole okra
	Salt & pepper, to taste

COMBINE all ingredients in a large pot.
BRING to a boil. **LOWER** heat.
SIMMER for 1 hour, **covered.**

Venison Stew Meat Soup
"Richard is a Dear"

1	pound venison stew meat, boiled
1	(8 ounce) can sliced mushrooms
1	can cream of mushroom soup
1	envelope dry onion soup mix
2	(14 ounce) cans chicken broth
	Salt & pepper, to taste

COMBINE all ingredients in a large pot.
BRING to a boil. **LOWER** heat.
SIMMER for 1 hour, **covered**.

www.anotherblondemoment.com

Venison Vegetable Soup
"Stued in Tupelo"

2	pounds venison stew meat, boiled, drained
2	cups water
1	quart apple cider
4	carrots, sliced
4	potatoes, peeled, cubed
4	celery stalks, chopped
1	onion, chopped
	Salt & pepper, to taste
6	dashes of hot sauce

COMBINE all ingredients in a large pot.
BRING to a boil. **LOWER** heat.
SIMMER for 2 hours, **covered**.

Q: What do you call a good looking man with a blonde?
A: A hostage.

---

www.anotherblondemoment.com

Browned Bag Doves
"Brown Bagging"

12	doves
	Salt & pepper
6	bacon slices, cut in half
1	can cream of mushroom soup
1	envelope dry onion soup mix
1½	cans water

SALT & **PEPPER** each dove.
WRAP each dove in bacon.
SECURE with toothpick.
PLACE dove in browning bag.
MIX last 3 ingredients. **POUR** in bag with dove.
PUNCH holes in top of bag.
PLACE in a 9x13 baking dish.
BAKE at 300 degrees for 2 hours.

Q: What's the 'redheads' mating call?
A: "Has the brunette left yet?"

---

www.anotherblondemoment.com

Slow-Cooked Doves
"Slow & Wingy"

8	doves
2	cups water
1	cup ketchup
4	Tablespoons Worcestershire
1	onion, sliced
3	bacon slices

STEAM 1st 2 ingredients in a large pan for 30 minutes, **covered**.
COMBINE all ingredients in a crock-pot.
COOK on **MEDIUM** for 3 hours.

Q: Why do brunettes like their hair color?
A: It doesn't show the dirt.

---

www.anotherblondemoment.com

Cajun Duck
"A Louisiana Quack"

3	duck breasts
3	cups water
1	(3 ounce) bag shrimp boil
3	bacon slices
½	stick margarine
1	teaspoon lemon juice

COMBINE 1st 3 ingredients in a large pot.
BRING to a boil for 30 minutes.
REMOVE ducks from water.
WRAP bacon around each duck breast.
SECURE with toothpick.
PLACE duck on rack in roasting pan with water.
MELT margarine in saucepan.
ADD lemon juice. **STIR.**
BAKE at 350 degrees for 15 minutes.
BASTE with lemon butter occasionally.

www.anotherblondemoment.com

Marmalade Duck
"A Preserved Quack"

6	**duck breasts**
⅔	**cup burgundy wine**
⅓	**cup soy sauce**
1	**stick margarine, melted**
1	**(6 ounce) jar orange marmalade**
1	**cup burgundy wine**

COMBINE 1st 3 ingredients in a large bowl.
MARINATE 1 day.
PLACE duck breast on hot grill, breast side up.
COMBINE last 3 ingredients in a bowl. **MIX** well.
COOK duck 3 minutes, **basting** with sauce.
TURN. **BASTE**. **COOK** 3 more minutes.
REPEAT 2 more times.

Q: Why is brunette an evil color?
A: When was the last time you saw a redheaded witch?

---

www.anotherblondemoment.com

Italian Venison Back Strap
"Saia is Strapped"

1	venison back strap, cut in ½ strips
½	cup sour cream
¼	cup brown mustard
1	cup Italian breadcrumbs
½	stick margarine
1	cup olive oil

WRAP back strap with plastic wrap.
POUND with mallet on both sides.
COMBINE next 2 ingredients in a bowl.
PLACE bread crumbs in a separate bowl.
DIP back strap in sour cream mixture.
COAT in breadcrumbs on both sides.
COMBINE last 2 ingredients in a skillet.
FRY back strap in hot oil for 5-10 minutes on each side.

Q: Why can't blondes 'tease' their hair?
A: Because it's not funny.

---

www.anotherblondemoment.com

Venison Burgers
"Regan is Dear"

2	pounds ground venison
4	bacon slices, cooked, crumbled
	Salt & pepper, to taste
1	(4 ounce) bleu cheese, room temperature
2	Tablespoons heavy cream
8	hamburger buns

COMBINE 1st 3 ingredients in a large bowl.
SHAPE into patties.
BEAT next 2 ingredients until smooth.
SPLIT each patty in half. (like butterflying)
SPREAD 1 Tablespoon cheese mixture in middle of each patty.
FOLD back together. Seal edges with fingers.
GRILL until desired doneness.
SERVE on buns.

> **Q: What's the true definition of a blonde?**
> **A:** Redhead. With the fire of passion missing.

www.anotherblondemoment.com

BBQ Venison Roast
"Blondequed & Roasted"

4	garlic cloves
	Salt & pepper, to taste
1	(12 ounce) beer
2	onions, sliced
2	cups barbecue sauce
2-3	pound venison roast

COMBINE 1st 5 ingredients in a large bowl.
PLACE venison in mixture. **MARINATE** 1 day.
PLACE all ingredients in a crock-pot.
COOK on **MEDIUM** for 8 hours.

Q: How do you get a redhead to argue with you?
A: You say something.

www.anotherblondemoment.com

Brown Sugar Venison Roast
"Sugar Coated Rump"

2-3	pound venison roast
¼	cup brown sugar
1	Tablespoon prepared mustard
1	Tablespoon liquid smoke
1	Tablespoon lemon juice
2	teaspoons Worcestershire
2	teaspoons celery salt
1	teaspoon garlic powder
¼	cup red wine

PLACE venison in a large roasting pan.
COMBINE remaining ingredients in a bowl.
POUR over venison roast.
BAKE at 350 degrees for 3 hours, **covered**.
BAKE for 30 more minutes, **uncovered**.
SERVE in juices from pan.

www.anotherblondemoment.com

Dijon Venison Steaks
"Is Cox at Stake?"

8	venison steak fillets
1	cup Dijon mustard
	Salt, to taste
	Pepper, to taste
1	cup flour
	Oil

DIP venison steaks in mustard.
COMBINE next 3 ingredients in separate bowl.
COAT venison in flour mixture.
FRY steaks in hot oil for 5-10 minutes on each side.

Q: What do you call going on a date with a brunette?
A: Brown bagging it.

Dove Smothered in Wild Rice
"Smothered in Wildness"

12	doves
1	onion, chopped
2	Tablespoons margarine
	Salt & pepper, to taste
1	can cream of celery soup
1	(4 ounce) can mushrooms, drained
1	teaspoon Kitchen Bouquet
1	cup sour cream
1	(6 ounce) box long grain wild rice, cooked

ARRANGE dove in a pam-sprayed 2-quart casserole dish.

SAUTE next 6 ingredients in a large skillet.

MIX well.

POUR mixture over doves.

BAKE at 350 degrees for 1 hour, **covered**.

TURN doves occasionally. **ADD** sour cream.

BAKE 20 more minutes, **uncovered**.

SPOON dove & sauce over rice.

Cheesy Duck Casserole
"Chip is a Cheesy Quack"

3	cups duck breasts, boiled, drained, chopped
2	cups shredded cheddar cheese
2	(14 ounce) cans chicken broth
1	onion, chopped
2	celery stalks, chopped
1/2	teaspoon pepper
1/2	teaspoon salt
1	can cream of mushroom soup
4	cups butter crackers, crumbled, reserve 1 cup

COMBINE all ingredients in a large bowl.
MIX well.
SPOON in a pam-sprayed 2-quart casserole dish.
SPRINKLE with reserved cracker crumbs.
BAKE at 350 degrees for 45 minutes.

www.anotherblondemoment.com

Venison Beans & Pasta
"Dear, Ground Me!"

2	pounds ground venison
1	onion, chopped
1	bell pepper, chopped
2	(15 ounce) cans kidney beans, drained
2	tomatoes, chopped
$2\frac{1}{2}$	teaspoons cornstarch to $2\frac{1}{2}$ teaspoons water
1	(14 ounce) can beef broth
1	(8 ounce) processed cheese, cubed
1	(12 ounce) Ziti pasta, cooked according to directions

SAUTE 1st 3 ingredients in a large pot.
ADD next 2 ingredients.
MIX cornstarch & water until smooth in a separate bowl.
ADD broth to cornstarch mixture.
ADD to venison mixture.
BOIL mixture for 1 minute. **TAKE** off heat.
STIR in last 2 ingredients.
POUR all ingredients in a pam-sprayed 2-quart casserole dish.
BAKE at 375 degrees for 20 minutes.

www.anotherblondemoment.com

Venison Noodle Bake
"Is it Limp, Dear?"

2	pounds ground venison
1	Tablespoon margarine
1	onion, chopped
1	bell pepper, chopped
2	(8 ounce) cans tomato sauce
1½	cups cottage cheese
½	cup sour cream
1	(8 ounce) cream cheese, softened
1	(8 ounce) bag wide egg noodles, cooked

SAUTE 1st 5 ingredients in a large skillet.
COMBINE next 3 ingredients in a separate bowl.
PLACE ½ the noodles in pam-sprayed 2-quart casserole dish.
LAYER cheese mixture, venison, noodles.
BAKE at 350 degrees for 45 minutes.

Venison Potato Bake
"Will He be Fried or Baked?"

1	pound ground venison
1	onion, chopped
	Pepper, to taste
1	can cheddar cheese soup
1	can cream of celery soup
1	(10 ounce) bag frozen French fries

SAUTE 1st 3 ingredients in a large skillet.
POUR in a pam-sprayed 9x13 baking dish.
MIX soups in separate bowl.
POUR soups over the venison.
COVER with frozen French fries.
BAKE at 350 degrees for 45 minutes, **covered**.

Crock-Pot Venison Rice
"A Slow-Cooked Dear"

1	pound ground venison
1	bell pepper, chopped
1	onion, chopped
1/2	cup whole grain rice, uncooked
4	tomatoes, chopped
6	American cheese slices

COMBINE all ingredients in a crock-pot.
MIX well. **COOK** on **LOW** for 8 hours.

www.anotherblondemoment.com

Venison Roast, Potatoes & Carrots
"Dakota Got Bagged & Roasted"

1	large oven cooking bag
2-3	pound venison roast
1	onion, quartered
2	potatoes, quartered
1	(8 ounce) bag mini carrots
2	Tablespoons liquid smoke
3	Tablespoons Worcestershire
3	Tablespoons soy sauce
1	(14 ounce) can beef broth

PLACE cooking bag in a 2-quart casserole dish.
ADD all ingredients inside cooking bag.
ADD water to bottom of casserole dish.
SEAL bag. **POKE** small holes in top of bag.
BAKE at 325 degrees for 3-4 hours.

Very good. Did not use bag. Slow cooker

Venison Sausage Bean Bake
"Did You Pork that Dear?"

1	**(20 ounce) can baked beans**
1	**onion, chopped**
2	**Tablespoons Karo syrup**
1	**teaspoon dry mustard**
	Salt & pepper, to taste
2	**pounds ground venison sausage**
½	**cup brown sugar**
1	**bell pepper, chopped**
1	**cup barbecue sauce**

COMBINE all ingredients in a large bowl.
MIX well.
POUR in a pam-sprayed 2-quart casserole.
BAKE at 350 degrees for 1 hour.

.

Q: Why did the blonde tip toe past the medicine cabinet?
A: So she wouldn't wake up the sleeping pills.

---

www.anotherblondemoment.com

Venison Macaroni
"Patrick gave Dakota, Moore"

1	Tablespoon olive oil
1	onion, chopped
1	garlic clove, chopped
2	pounds ground venison sausage
3	cups macaroni, cooked according to directions
1	(28 ounce) can crushed tomatoes
1	Tablespoon oregano
1	Tablespoon basil
3	cups shredded cheddar cheese

SAUTE 1st 4 ingredients in a large skillet.
COMBINE all ingredients in a large bowl.
POUR in a pam-sprayed 2-quart casserole dish.
BAKE at 325 degrees for 20 minutes.

Q: What is dumber than a brunette building a fire under the water?
A: A blonde trying to put it out.

www.anotherblondemoment.com

Venison Pepper Steak
"Sherried & Peppered"

1	cup flour
	Salt & pepper, to taste
2	pounds venison steak, thinly sliced, pounded
1	onion, sliced
1	bell pepper, sliced
2	tomatoes, chopped

COMBINE 1st 2 ingredients in a large bowl.
DIP steak in seasoned flour on both sides.
BROWN steak in a skillet with margarine.
PLACE all ingredients in pam-sprayed 2-quart casserole dish.
BAKE at 350 degrees for 2 hours. **REMOVE**.
THICKEN gravy with flour & water.

Q: Why are there not many brunette jokes?
A: Because blondes would have to think them up.

---

www.anotherblondemoment.com

How to 'CATCH' a Mate

RECIPES for 'CATCHING'

'Snagging the Pearl Pizza'

1	acceptance to a date
2	movie tickets for a romantic-comedy
3-4	adventurous outings
1	semi-serious conversation about yourself
	Lots of 'gestural dancing'
	A splash of text or phone

DON'T set expectations too high.
ADD positiveness to whatever activity.
BE adventurous. Fishing, Hunting, Biking.
ROLL & FLATTEN OUT the conversation.
(Your life, beliefs, likes & dislikes).
LAYER with similarly synchronized body
movements. Ex: Toasting, same time drinking.
DON'T overuse the phone.
REMOVE quickly from situation if conversations
become to thick.

• Watch for **Pupil Dilation**
• Watch for **Pulse & Blood Pressure** increases
• Watch for **Blushing & Rapid Breathing**
• Watch for **Posturing**

www.anotherblondemoment.com

RECIPES for 'CATCHING'

'Reeling in the Catch' Cobbler

Several conversations about family
2-3 Day Trips
Group Dates with friends
A lot of great listening skills
Several sincere compliments

ROLL out conversation about family &
background.
(Set aside for later)
ADD 2-3 day trips to get to know each other
better.
COMBINE several group dates to taste.
COMBINE listening skills & compliments.
PUT the life & family conversation in crock-pot.
COOK on **LOW** heat for many months.

- **HUMOUR** adds likeability
- **HUMOUR** adds trust
- **HUMOUR** adds attraction
- **JUDICIOUS HUMOUR** reduces anxiety and
  establishes a relaxed mood

Seafood Recipes
(Crab, Crawfish, Fish, Oysters, Salmon, Shrimp, Tuna)

How to 'CATCH' a Mate
(RECIPES for 'CATCHING')

www.anotherblondemoment.com

Seafood Recipes
(Crab, Crawfish, Fish, Oysters, Salmon, Shrimp, Tuna)

www.anotherblondemoment.com

Crabmeat Cheese Dip
"A Processed Chipper"

1	(16 ounce) processed cheese
2	(6 ounce) cans crabmeat, drained
1	bunch of green onions, chopped
$1\frac{1}{2}$	cups mayonnaise
$\frac{1}{2}$	teaspoon seasoned salt
$\frac{1}{2}$	teaspoon pepper

MELT cheese in microwave until creamy.
ADD remaining ingredients. **STIR**.
SERVE hot with crackers.

Crabmeat Dijon Dip
"Tara has Sparked Me"

3	(6 ounce) cans crabmeat
1	bell pepper, chopped
1	(4 ounce) jar diced pimientos
1	Tablespoon Dijon mustard
2	eggs, beaten
1	cup mayonnaise

MIX all ingredients in a large bowl.
POUR in a pam-sprayed 9x9 baking dish.
BAKE at 350 degrees for 20 minutes.
SERVE with crackers.

www.anotherblondemoment.com

Crabmeat Horseradish Dip
"Christy's Horsing Around for a Chip"

½	teaspoon cream-style horseradish
¼	teaspoon salt
1	(8 ounce) cream cheese, softened
1	Tablespoon milk
1	(6 ounce) can crabmeat, drained
2	Tablespoons onion, chopped

COMBINE all ingredients in a bowl.
POUR in a pam-sprayed 9x13 baking dish.
BAKE at 375 degrees for 15 minutes.
SERVE hot with rye bread.

Smoked Oyster Cheese Ball
"Tracey Paid a Price'"

1	(8 ounce) cream cheese, softened
1	(3 ounce) can smoked oysters, drained
1	Tablespoon Worcestershire
½	teaspoon garlic powder
1	teaspoon curry powder
¾	cup pecans, chopped

MASH 1st 2 ingredients with a fork in a bowl.
ADD next 3 ingredients. **MIX** well.
SHAPE in a ball. **REFRIGERATE** until hard.
ROLL ball in pecans. **SERVE** with crackers.

www.anotherblondemoment.com

Salmon Loaf
"A Loaf of Benji Man"

1	(15 ounce) can salmon, drained
1	Tablespoon oil
1	teaspoon lemon juice
2	bread slices, crumbled
2	eggs, beaten
3	Tablespoons ketchup
1	onion, chopped
	Salt, to taste
	Pepper, to taste

COMBINE all ingredients in a large bowl.
POUR in a pam-sprayed loaf pan.
BAKE at 350 degrees for 35-40 minutes.
SERVE with crackers.

Shrimp Dill Dip
"Ashley is a Dilly"

1	(8 ounce) cream cheese, softened
1/4	cup mayonnaise
1	Tablespoon parsley
1/2	teaspoon dried dill weed
2	(6 ounce) cans shrimp, drained
1	Tablespoon lemon juice

COMBINE all ingredients in a bowl. **CHILL**.
SERVE with crackers or vegetables.

www.anotherblondemoment.com

Shrimp Italian Dip
"Italian or Geek?"

2	(6 ounce) cans shrimp, drained
1	envelope dry Italian seasoning mix
1	(8 ounce) cream cheese, softened
1	(12 ounce) sour cream
1	teaspoon lemon juice
1	teaspoon Cavendar's Greek seasoning

COMBINE all ingredients in a bowl. **CHILL**.
SERVE with Fritos.

Shrimp Crescents
"I'm all Sealed Up"

1	(14 ounce) can artichoke hearts, drained, chopped
1	(4 ounce) can diced green chilies
1	cup grated Parmesan cheese
¼	cup mayonnaise
32	small shrimp, cooked, peeled
2	(8 ounce) cans crescent dinner rolls

COMBINE 1st 5 ingredients in a bowl. **MIX** well.
UNROLL crescent rolls.
CUT each dough in half lengthwise.
SPOON mixture into dough. **SEAL**.
PLACE dough on pam-sprayed cookie sheet.
BAKE at 350 degrees for 10-15 minutes.

www.anotherblondemoment.com

Tuna Smoke Spread
"Smokin' & Spreadin'"

3/4	cup Italian dressing
1	cup sour cream
1/2	teaspoon seasoned salt
1	Tablespoon minced onion
1	teaspoon liquid smoke
1	(6 ounce) can tuna, drained, flaked

COMBINE all ingredients in a bowl. **MIX** well.
REFRIGERATE 1 hour. **SERVE** with crackers.

Crabmeat Cilantro Salad
"Crabby Mexican Parsley"

1	pound fresh crabmeat or 2 (6 ounce) cans crabmeat
1/2	cup red onion, chopped
4	Tablespoons cilantro
1	(3 ounce) cream cheese, softened
4	Tablespoons mayonnaise
3	Tablespoons lemon juice

COMBINE all ingredients in a bowl. **MIX** well.
SPOON on a bed of lettuce.

www.anotherblondemoment.com

Crabmeat Egg Salad
"He is Egging Me On"

2   **cups fresh crabmeat or 2 cans crabmeat**
2   **eggs, hard-boiled, sliced**

PLACE ¼ cup crabmeat on bed of lettuce with egg slice.

DRESSING:
½   **cup crabmeat**
1   **cup mayonnaise**
1   **cup heavy cream**
¼   **cup chili sauce**
1   **teaspoon Worcestershire**
2   **Tablespoons lemon juice**
1   **teaspoon Cavendar's Greek seasoning**

MIX all dressing ingredients in a large bowl.
CHILL.
SPOON 2 Tablespoons of dressing over crabmeat.

Q: What is a redhead?
A: A blonde with an attitude.

---

www.anotherblondemoment.com

Crawfish Creole Salad
"Honey, I'm Tossing for You"

DRESSING:

6	Tablespoons Creole mustard
1½	Tablespoons lemon juice
1½	Tablespoons honey
1	teaspoon Blonde all-purpose seasoning
1	teaspoon olive oil
	Salt & pepper, to taste

COMBINE all ingredients in a bowl. **MIX** well.

SALAD:

6	cups romaine lettuce
2	cups crawfish tail meat, cooked
2	Tablespoons sunflower seed kernels, toasted
1	(4 ounce) can sliced black olives, drained
1	egg, hard-boiled, sliced
1	Tablespoon Cavendar's Greek seasoning

COMBINE all salad ingredients in a large bowl.
TOSS with dressing.
SERVE.

www.anotherblondemoment.com

Crawfish Pasta Salad
"Emily is Crawfishing Me"

1	pound crawfish tail meat
1	stick margarine
1	bunch of green onions, chopped
2	teaspoons Creole seasoning
1	pint half-n-half cream
1	(12 ounce) package pasta, cooked according to directions

SAUTÉ 1st 3 ingredients in a large skillet for 5 minutes.
ADD next 2 ingredients for 5 minutes.
STIR occasionally.
COOK for 5-10 more minutes over medium heat.
ADD cooked pasta,
STIR on low heat for 8 minutes.
SERVE hot.

Q: What's the difference between a terrorist and a redhead?
A: You can negotiate with a terrorist.

---

www.anotherblondemoment.com

Shrimp Herb & Garlic Pasta Salad
"Jaxon's 1st Beach Cooking"

2	teaspoons olive oil
2	pounds shrimp, uncooked, peeled
1	bottle Lawry's herb & garlic marinade, with lemon juice
¼	cup green onions, chopped
2	teaspoons Cavendar's Greek seasoning
1	(12 ounce) pasta, cooked according to directions

SAUTÉ 1st 5 ingredients in a large skillet for 5-10 minutes.
ADD cooked pasta.
STIR on low heat for 8-10 minutes.
SERVE hot or cold.

BLONDES IN THE AIR!

There were two blondes going to California for the summer. They were about two hours into the flight and the pilot gets on the intercom and says, "We just lost an engine but it is all right we have three more but it will take us an hour longer."

A half hour later he gets on the intercom again and says, "We just lost another engine but it's all right we have two more it will take us another half hour though."

One of the blondes said, "If we lose the two last engines we will be up here all day."

---

www.anotherblondemoment.com

Shrimp Remoulade Pasta
"Orange Beach Bungalow's Shrimped"

1½	cups mayonnaise
½	cup Dijon mustard
¼	cup ketchup
4	teaspoons horseradish
2	teaspoons Worcestershire
3	Tablespoons lemon juice
1	teaspoon hot sauce
1	(8 ounce) bag pasta, cooked according to directions
2	pounds shrimp, boiled, peeled, cut in half

COMBINE all ingredients in a large bowl. **TOSS.**
SERVE hot or cold.

Q: What's the difference between a blonde and a redhead?
A: A blonde is a redhead with all the fire burned out.
Redheads are just Blondes with high blood
pressure.

---

www.anotherblondemoment.com

Shrimp Tangy Salad
"Tammy is Tangy at 205"

3	cups shrimp, boiled, peeled, chopped
1	cup celery, chopped
4	eggs, hard-boiled, chopped
1/2	cup green olives, sliced
1/4	cup sweet onions, chopped
1/4	cup dill pickles, chopped
1	cup mayonnaise
2	Tablespoons chili sauce
1	Tablespoon horseradish

COMBINE all ingredients in a large bowl.
TOSS. **SERVE** on a bed of lettuce.

Shrimp & Rice Salad
"Peking got Shrimped"

1	pound small shrimp, boiled, peeled
1	(15 ounce) can cut green beans, drained
1	(4 ounce) can sliced black olives
1/3	cup green onions, chopped
1/2	cup Italian dressing
3	Tablespoons chili sauce
1/4	teaspoon pepper
1/8	teaspoon garlic powder
1 1/2	cups rice, cooked

COMBINE all ingredients in a large bowl.
TOSS. **SERVE**.

www.anotherblondemoment.com

Tuna Feta Salad
"Angel Tuna"

2	(15 ounce) cans navy beans, rinsed, drained
1	(6 ounce) can tuna, drained
½	cup crumbled feta cheese
½	cup red onion, chopped
⅓	cup olive oil
3	Tablespoons balsamic vinegar

COMBINE all ingredients in a large bowl.
MIX well.
REFRIGERATE. SERVE on a bed of lettuce.

Crabmeat Asparagus Soup
"Miss Lucille Gossiped"

1	can cream of mushroom soup
1	can cream of asparagus soup
2	(14 ounce) cans evaporated milk
1	cup half-n-half cream
1	cup fresh crabmeat or 2 cans crabmeat
	Salt & pepper, to taste

COMBINE all ingredients in a medium saucepan.
BRING to a boil. **REDUCE** heat.
SIMMER for 30 minutes. **SERVE.**

www.anotherblondemoment.com

Crawfish Corn Bisque
"Slow-Cooked Corny Sentell"

2	cans cream of potato soup
1	can cream of mushroom soup
1	(15 ounce) can whole kernel corn
1	pound crawfish tail meat
1	pint half-n-half cream
1	(3 ounce) cream cheese, softened

COMBINE all in ingredients in a crock-pot.
COOK on **HIGH** for 3 hours.
SERVE over rice.

Crawfish Cheese Soup
"A Sandy Destin Donna"

1	(8 ounce) cream cheese, softened
1	stick margarine
½	cup green onions, chopped
2	cans cream of potato soup
1	(15 ounce) can shoe peg corn
1	(15 ounce) can cream-style corn
2	cups milk
2	teaspoons Creole seasoning
1	pound crawfish tail meat

COMBINE all ingredients in a large saucepan.
BRING to a boil. **REDUCE** heat.
SIMMER for 1 hour, **covered**.

www.anotherblondemoment.com

Oyster Soup
"Creamy Aphrodisiac"

1	quart shucked oysters, with juice
1	stick margarine
1½	quarts milk
1	cup heavy cream
¼	cup chopped parsley
	Salt & pepper, to taste

COMBINE all ingredients in a large saucepan.
BRING to a boil. **REDUCE** heat.
SIMMER for 1 hour, **covered**.

Salmon Bisque
"Is Paul Sal Manned?"

1	(14 ounce) can chicken broth
1	(8 ounce) can Alaska pink salmon, drained
1	(10 ounce) jar mild chunky salsa
½	cup nonfat dill dip
	Salt, to taste
	Pepper, to taste

COMBINE all ingredients in a medium saucepan.
BRING to a boil. **REDUCE** heat.
SIMMER for 1 hour, **covered**.

www.anotherblondemoment.com

Seafood Gumbo
"Peggy on My Mind"

½	stick margarine
4	Tablespoons flour
2	quarts water
1	(16 ounce) bag frozen whole okra
6	tomatoes, diced
½	cup minced onion
1	pound shrimp, peeled
1	pound crabmeat
1	pint fresh oysters, with juice

BLEND 1st 3 ingredients in a large pot.
STIR until paste-like roux (that would be smooth).
ADD next 3 ingredients. **STIR**.
COOK on low heat for 50-60 minutes.
ADD last 3 ingredients when roux turns a rich brown color.
COOK on medium low heat for 30 minutes.
SERVE over rice.

Q: Do you know why blondes have more fun?
A: Because there is not enough redheads around.

---

www.anotherblondemoment.com

Shrimp Soup
"The Foxy Flamingo Shrimp"

1	cup green onions, chopped
2	celery stalks, chopped
3	Tablespoons margarine
1	can cream of shrimp soup
1	can milk
1	can cream of celery soup
1	can water
	Pepper, to taste
1	pound shrimp, peeled, chopped

SAUTÉ 1st 3 ingredients in a medium pot.
ADD last 6 ingredients. **STIR.**
SIMMER for 1 hour. **STIR** occasionally.

BIMBABBLE - Noises coming from a group of blondes trying to hold a conservation.

Shrimp & Corn Soup
"An Drew His Corny Lane"

2	(15 ounce) cans cream-style corn
1	(15 ounce) can whole kernel corn
1	(10 ounce) can diced Rotel tomatoes
1	(8 ounce) can tomato sauce
2	celery stalks, chopped
4	cups water
1	can cream of celery soup
2	Tablespoons Creole seasoning
2	pounds raw shrimp, peeled, cut up

COMBINE 1st 8 ingredients in a crock-pot.
COOK on **LOW** for 7 hours. **ADD** shrimp.
STIR. **TURN** crock-pot on **HIGH** for 45 minutes.

IN SEARCH OF?

I looked into a blonde's eyes, but all I saw was the back of her head!

---

www.anotherblondemoment.com

Shrimp Cheese Soup
"Joy & Zoe got Creamed"

1	stick margarine
1	bunch green onions
1	(8 ounce) cream cheese, cut into cubes
2	cans cream of potato soup
2	pounds shrimp, peeled
1	can cream of mushroom soup
2	pints half-n-half cream
2	(15 ounce) cans whole kernel corn
2	Tablespoons Creole seasoning

SAUTÉ 1st 2 ingredients in a large pot.
ADD remaining ingredients. **STIR** occasionally.
SIMMER for 1 hour.

BIMBELLOW - A sound emanating from a blonde after she finally got the most recent blonde joke she heard.

Shrimp & Rice Soup
"Mark it Louie for Shrimp!"

4	cups water
4	chicken bouillon cubes
1	(6 ounce) box long grain wild rice
2	celery stalks, chopped
2	cans chicken and rice soup
2	cans cream of shrimp soup
2	cups milk
2	(6 ounce) cans shrimp, drained
1	cup sour cream

COMBINE 1st 7 ingredients in a large pot.
SIMMER for 45 minutes.
ADD last 2 ingredients.
SIMMER for 10 more minutes.

BIMBOIL - A condition of a blonde as she hears a blonde joke being told that she doesn't understand yet.

---

www.anotherblondemoment.com

Shrimpy Wine Soup
"Wicked Wanda Whined the Shrimp"

3	(14 ounce) cans chicken broth
2	Tablespoons hot sauce
½	cup green onions, chopped
2	celery stalks, chopped
1	cup fresh parsley
1	Tablespoon garlic salt
1	Tablespoon Worcestershire
2	cups dry white wine
2	pounds shrimp, peeled

COMBINE all ingredients in a large pot.
BRING to a boil. **REDUCE** heat.
SIMMER for 1 hour, **covered**.
ADD shrimp. **SIMMER** for 30 more minutes.

BIMBAFFLED - A constant mental state of blondes.

---

www.anotherblondemoment.com

Corn Chip Fish
"Chip is Corny & Fishy"

1	cup mayonnaise
2	Tablespoons lime juice
	Salt, to taste
	Pepper, to taste
4	fish fillets, (any kind of fish) rinsed, dried
1½	cups corn chips, crushed

COMBINE 1st 2 ingredients in a bowl.
SALT & PEPPER fish fillets.
DIP fillets in mayonnaise mixture.
PLACE crushed corn chips on wax paper.
COAT both sides of fish in chips.
PLACE fillets on a foil-covered baking sheet.
BAKE at 425 degrees for 15 minutes or until fish flakes.

BIMBOBBLE - A blonde playing catch.

---

www.anotherblondemoment.com

Lemon Parmesan Fish
"Ellie James, Oh My Goodness"

½	cup Parmesan cheese
¼	cup margarine, softened
3	Tablespoons mayonnaise
2	Tablespoons lemon juice
¼	teaspoon dried basil
¼	teaspoon pepper
⅛	teaspoon onion powder
⅛	teaspoon celery salt
2	pounds fish fillets (any kind of fish)

COMBINE 1st 8 ingredients in a bowl. **MIX** well.
PLACE fillets on a foil-covered baking sheet.
BROIL for 5 minutes on each side.
REMOVE fillets from the oven.
COVER fillets with Parmesan mixture.
BROIL 5 more minutes or until fish flakes.

BIMBLOOPER - General result of a blonde's actions.

---

www.anotherblondemoment.com

Flounder Cilantro Fillets
"Will Floundered Around"

2	pounds flounder fillets (about 6-8)
²/₃	cup margarine
3	Tablespoons fresh cilantro
1	Tablespoon lime juice
1	Tablespoon lemon juice
1	Tablespoon Cavendar's Greek seasoning

PLACE fillets on foil-covered baking sheet.
BROIL 5 minutes. **TURN** fillets over.
BROIL 5 minutes until flounder flakes.
COMBINE last 5 ingredients in a saucepan. **HEAT**.
STIR. SPOON over flounder just before serving.

BIMBULB - A very dim blonde light bulb.

www.anotherblondemoment.com

Flounder Parmesan Fillets
"Don't Flounder Mi, Gi!"

2	cups mayonnaise
2	pounds flounder fillets (about 6-8)
2	cups bread crumbs
1	cup grated Parmesan cheese
1	teaspoon salt
1	teaspoon pepper

PUT mayonnaise in an oblong dish.
COAT fillets with mayonnaise.
COMBINE last 4 ingredients in a separate bowl.
DIP flounder in bread crumb mixture. **COAT.**
PLACE in pam-sprayed shallow baking dish.
BAKE at 375 degrees for 25 minutes, **uncovered**.

BIMBILLION - A blonde giving an estimate of anything.

---

www.anotherblondemoment.com

Grouper Tequila
"Prissy Cilla Shot Tequila"

FRUIT SALSA:

1	(8 ounce) can diced pineapple
1	cup fresh strawberries, sliced
2	green onions, chopped
	Fresh cilantro to taste
1	lime, juiced
2	Tablespoons diced jalapeño peppers

COMBINE all ingredients in a bowl.

½	cup lime juice
¼	cup tequila
2	Tablespoons cilantro, chopped
1	garlic clove, chopped
4	grouper fillets
	Fruit salsa (see above)

MIX 1st 4 ingredients in a large bowl.
PLACE fillets in lime mixture.
PLACE fillets on a hot grill. **BASTE** with lime.
GRILL until grouper flakes with a fork.
TAKE off grill. **SPOON** fruit salsa over fillets.

www.anotherblondemoment.com

Salmon Dijon
"A Petered Sal Man"

2	cups Dijon mustard
4	skinless salmon fillets
½	cup bread crumbs
4	Tablespoons dried parsley
½	cup walnuts, chopped
1	stick margarine, melted

SPREAD mustard generously over fillets.
MIX remaining ingredients in a bowl.
PLACE fillets in a pam-sprayed 9x13 dish.
POUR bread crumb mixture over salmon.
BAKE at 450 degrees for 20 minutes or until salmon flakes.

BIMBLAZE - The result of a blonde trying to cook.

---

www.anotherblondemoment.com

Grilled Shrimp
"Barbie's Qued"

½	cup olive oil
2	Tablespoons lemon juice
1	teaspoon minced garlic
	Pinch of red pepper
½	cup chili sauce
2	Tablespoons Worcestershire
½	teaspoon salt
½	teaspoon pepper
2	pounds jumbo shrimp, peeled

COMBINE 1st 8 ingredients in a large bowl.
STIR. ADD shrimp. **REFRIGERATE** for 1 hour.
POUR marinade in separate bowl from shrimp.
SKEWER shrimp. **BASTE** with extra marinade.
GRILL 6 minutes on each side. **TURN**.

Spicy Shrimp
"Juiced & Spicy"

2	pounds shrimp, cooked, peeled
3	limes, juiced
1	lemon, juiced
1	red onion, chopped
1	cucumber, peeled, chopped
1	tomato, chopped
1	jalapeño pepper, chopped
1	cup fresh cilantro
2	Tablespoons olive oil

COMBINE all ingredients in a large bowl.
REFRIGERATE for 2 hours.
SERVE.

Snapper Creole
"Neppie just Snapped"

1	stick margarine, melted
4	Tablespoons lemon juice
2	pounds red snapper fillets
4	teaspoons Creole seasoning
2	teaspoons Cavendar's Greek seasoning
½	cup sliced almonds

COMBINE 1st 2 ingredients in a medium bowl.
COAT fillets in margarine mixture.
PLACE fillets in a 9x13 baking dish.
SPRINKLE fillets with next 2 ingredients.
BAKE at 375 degrees for 25 minutes or until fish flakes.
SPRINKLE almonds over fish for 5 minutes.

www.anotherblondemoment.com

Snapper Curried-Style
"My Brain Booster is Snapping"

2	**pounds red snapper**
1	**onion, chopped**
2	**celery stalks, chopped**
2	**Tablespoons margarine**
2	**teaspoons curry powder**
½	**cup milk**

PLACE snapper in a pam-sprayed 9x13 dish.
SAUTÉ next 4 ingredients in a skillet.
REMOVE from heat. **STIR** in milk.
POUR mixture over snapper.
BAKE at 350 degrees for 25 minutes.

BIMBOETTE - A young blonde.

www.anotherblondemoment.com

Tuna Teriyaki
"Belynda Tunaed Howard"

1	cup teriyaki sauce
3/4	cup olive oil
2	Tablespoons minced garlic
1	teaspoon pepper
1	teaspoon salt
4	yellow fin tuna fillets

COMBINE 1st 5 ingredients in a large sealable plastic bag.
PLACE tuna in bag. **SEAL** bag. **SHAKE** bag.
MARINATE in refrigerator for 1 hour.
PLACE tuna on hot grill. **BASTE** with teriyaki.
GRILL until desired doneness.

BIMBOOZLE - To fool a blonde.

---

www.anotherblondemoment.com

Crabmeat Casserole
"Are You a Crab, Cowart?"

1	stick margarine, divided 3 Tablespoons, 2 Tablespoons, melted
1/3	cup flour
1/4	teaspoon dry mustard
	Salt & pepper, to taste
2	cups half-n-half cream
1	egg, beaten
2 1/2	cups crabmeat
2	bread slices, torn
1	cup shredded Swiss cheese

COMBINE 1st 5 ingredients in a large skillet.
COOK on medium heat. **STIR** until thick.
STIR in next 2 ingredients.
POUR in a pam-sprayed 9x13 baking dish.
BAKE at 350 degrees for 15 minutes.
COMBINE last 2 ingredients with margarine.
POUR over crabmeat mixture.
BAKE 5 more minutes.

Crawfish Pasta
"Alex & Chel got Crawfished"

1	**pound crawfish tail meat**
1	**stick of butter (Do not use margarine)**
1	**pint of half-n-half cream**
1	**bunch green onions, chopped**
2	**Tablespoons Creole seasoning**
1	**(8 ounce) pasta, cooked according to directions**

SAUTÉ 1st 5 ingredients in a large pot.
COOK for 10 minutes over medium heat.
ADD pasta. **TOSS. SIMMER** for 10 minutes.
SERVE immediately.

BIMBORE – A blonde who uses "like" more than 10 times in a sentence.

---

www.anotherblondemoment.com

Salmon Fettuccini Toss
"Eric Baked Kelly"

3	Tablespoons olive oil
½	cup onion, chopped
2	Tablespoons Italian seasoning
½	cup pitted kalamata olives
1	(14 ounce) can red salmon, drained
1	(8 ounce) sour cream
1	(8 ounce) plain yogurt
1	cup blue cheese, crumbled
1	(8 ounce) fettuccini noodles, cooked according to directions

SAUTÉ 1st 5 ingredients in a large pot.
COOK on low heat for 10 minutes.
STIR in next 3 ingredients. **ADD** pasta. **TOSS.**
SERVE warm.

BIMBROWNIE - A well-tanned blonde.

Seafood Lasagna
"Larry Got Layered"

2	Tablespoons margarine
1	onion, chopped
1	(8 ounce) package cream cheese, softened
1	(15 ounce) ricotta cheese
1	(4 ounce) jar diced pimientos
1	egg, beaten
1	can cream of shrimp soup
1	can fiesta nacho cheese soup
1/4	cup milk
1/3	cup white wine
1	pound small shrimp, cooked, peeled
2	(6 ounce) cans crabmeat, drained
8	lasagna noodles, cooked according to directions
1/2	cup grated Parmesan cheese
1	cup shredded cheddar cheese

SAUTÉ 1st 2 ingredients in a large saucepan.
ADD next 4 ingredients until creamy.
HEAT next 6 ingredients in separate saucepan.
PLACE noodles in pam-sprayed 9x13 baking dish.
SPREAD half cream cheese mixture on noodles.
TOP with half seafood mixture. **REPEAT.**
SPRINKLE Parmesan cheese on top.
BAKE at 350 degrees for 50-60 minutes.
REMOVE from oven. **TOP** with cheddar cheese.
RETURN to oven for 3 more minutes.

www.anotherblondemoment.com

Sun-Dried Tomato Shrimp
"Olivia is Swayze Shrimped?"

2	pounds shrimp, boiled, peeled
1	green bell pepper, chopped
1	red bell pepper, chopped
4	Tablespoons olive oil
2	teaspoons minced garlic
1	cup sun-dried tomato pesto
1	(8 ounce) whipping cream
1	cup grated Parmesan cheese
1	(12 ounce) pasta, cooked according to directions

SAUTÉ 1st 4 ingredients in a large saucepan.
ADD garlic after shrimp is almost cooked.
ADD sun-dried tomato pesto. **STIR** well.
ADD whipping cream. **ADD** parmesan cheese.
ADD cooked pasta. **MIX** together. **SERVE**.

BIMBRUNETTE - A blonde who dyes her hair brunette, usually to appear smarter than she actually is.

Shrimp & Yellow Rice
"Uno, Doce, Trey"

2	**(5 ounce) bags yellow rice, cooked according to directions**
1	**pound processed cheese, melted with rice**
¼	**cup onion, chopped**
1	**(10 ounce) can diced Rotel tomatoes**
2	**cans cream of mushroom soup**
2	**pounds shrimp, peeled**

MIX all ingredients in a large bowl.
POUR in a pam-sprayed 9x13 baking dish.
BAKE at 350 degrees for 45 minutes.

Tuna Casserole
"He is Tunaed & Rolled"

1	**(4 ounce) jar diced pimientos**
2	**cans cream of celery soup**
2	**(6 ounce) cans tuna, drained**
1	**cup milk**
1	**cup cheddar cheese**
1	**(8 ounce) pasta, cooked according to directions**

COMBINE all ingredients in a large bowl.
POUR in a pam-sprayed 9x13 baking dish.
BAKE at 350 degrees for 30 minutes.

www.anotherblondemoment.com

How to 'STEER' a Mate

RECIPES for 'DATING'

'Cheesy Dating Dip'

2	cups of grated space
6	cans of trust
9	acts of random kindness
5	exchanges of kisses
3	fun nights together a week
1	spiritual gathering a week

MELT grated space into 2 separate places.

ADD can of trust throughout relationship.

SLICE in a sweet text, a dress up night, a cooking night, a picnic, a card in the mail, a sweet email, a romantic get-away.

EXCHANGE several kisses while on together time.

COMBINE church, fellowship with other Christians, Bible study, meditations or prayers during the week.

'DATING,' the Kisses

Butterfly Kiss - With your faces less than a breath away, open and close your eyelids.

Cheek Kiss - With your hands on your partner's shoulders, gently brush your lips across the cheek.

Earlobe Kiss - Gently sip and suck the earlobe. Avoid loud sucking noises.

Eskimo Kiss - With your faces less than a breath apart, gently rub your noses together.

Eye Kiss - Hold your partner's head with both hands and slowly move their head in the direction you wish your kiss to go. Slowly kiss up towards your partner's eyes and give them a tender kiss on top of their closed eyes.

Eyelid Kiss - While your partner is resting or sleeping, very gently kiss the spot right below their brow bone.

Finger Kiss - Gently suck on their fingers.

Foot Kiss - Gently suck the toes and then lightly kiss the feet.

Forehead Kiss - Brush your lips lightly across the crown of their head.

Freeze Kiss - Put a small piece of ice in your mouth, then open mouth and kiss your partner, passing them the ice with your tongue.

French Kiss - Slowly move tongue around in a circle. (No Lizard)

Fruity Kiss - Take a small piece of fruit and place between your lips. Kiss your partner and nibble one half of the piece of fruit while they nibble the other until it breaks in half, allow the juice to run into your mouths.

Hand Kiss - Gently raise her hand to your lips. Lightly brush your lips across the top of her hand.

Hickey Kiss - The object is not to draw blood, but to gently leave a mark that will prove your interlude was not a dream.

Hostage Kiss - Cover your lips with tape. When they come close to you make noises like you're trying to tell them something and motion as if you can't get the tape off.

Beef Recipes
(Ground Beef, Roast, Steak)

How to 'STEER' a Mate
(RECIPES for 'DATING')

www.anotherblondemoment.com

Beef Recipes
(Ground Beef, Roast, Steak)

Corned Beef Bagel Dip
"Beef Up! Kay"

1½	cups mayonnaise
1½	cups sour cream
2	(5 ounce) sliced corned beef, chopped
2	Tablespoons onion, chopped
2	Tablespoons parsley
1	teaspoon seasoned salt
4	teaspoons prepared horseradish
1	teaspoon Cavendar's Greek seasoning
8	bagels, cut into bite-size pieces

MIX 1st 8 ingredients in a serving bowl. **CHILL**.
SERVE with bagels.

Dried Beef Dip
"Will You Take a Beefy Dip?"

1	(8 ounce) cream cheese, softened
2	teaspoons minced onions
2	teaspoons milk
	Dash of pepper
½	cup sour cream
1	(2½ ounce) jar dried beef, chopped

COMBINE all ingredients in a bowl. **MIX** well.
SPOON in a pam-sprayed pie plate.
BAKE at 350 degrees for 15-20 minutes.
SERVE with crackers.

www.anotherblondemoment.com

Dried Beef Wine Dip
"A Blonde Beef Whiner"

1	Tablespoon margarine, melted
2	Tablespoons dry white wine
1	(8 ounce) cream cheese, softened
1/2	cup sour cream
1	(2½ ounce) jar dried beef, chopped
1/2	cup pecans, chopped

COMBINE all ingredients in a bowl. **MIX** well.
SERVE with crackers.

Beef Cheese Roll-Ups
"Roll His Beef Up!

1	pound ground beef
1	envelope dry onion soup mix
1	Tablespoon Cavendar's Greek seasoning
2	(8 ounce) cans crescent rolls
1	cup shredded cheddar cheese
1	cup shredded Monterey Jack cheese

BROWN 1st 3 ingredients in a skillet. **DRAIN**.
CUT each perforated dough in half.
SPOON 1 teaspoon beef mixture in dough.
ADD cheeses. **ROLL** up.
BAKE at 375 degrees for 10-12 minutes.

www.anotherblondemoment.com

Beef Mini Pizzas
"Kurt His Beef"

1	**pound ground beef**
1	**pound hot sausage**
1	**(16 ounce) processed cheese, cubed**
1	**teaspoon oregano**
1	**teaspoon parsley**
2	**loaves party rye bread**

BROWN 1st 2 ingredients in a skillet. **DRAIN.**
PLACE all ingredients in bowl, except bread.
PUT into microwave and cook until cheese melts.
PLACE a tablespoon of beef mixture on bread.
PLACE bread on cookie sheet.
BROIL for 3-5 minutes.

BIMBLANK - Frequent blonde facial expression.

---

www.anotherblondemoment.com

Beef Taco Dip
Is it Hart or Law?

1	**pound ground beef**
1	**envelope dry taco seasoning mix**
³⁄₄	**cup water**

BROWN above ingredients in a skillet. **DRAIN.**

1	**(12 ounce) bag scoops corn chips**
2	**cups shredded cheddar cheese**
2	**medium tomatoes, chopped**
¹⁄₂	**cup sour cream**

ARRANGE scoops on a cookie sheet.
SPOON 1 teaspoon of meat mixture in chip.
SPRINKLE with cheese. **BROIL** for 5 minutes.
TOP with tomato & sour cream.

BIMBLARNEY – A result of a blonde bragging about herself.

---

www.anotherblondemoment.com

Beef Tortilla Wedges
"Will Mary John be Beefed?"

1	**pound ground beef**
1	**envelope dry taco seasoning mix**
¾	**cup water**
1	**Tablespoon oil**
4	**(6 inch) corn tortillas**
1	**(16 ounce) can refried beans**
1	**cup shredded cheddar cheese**
2	**tomatoes, chopped**
1	**(4 ounce) can diced green chilies**

BROWN 1st 3 ingredients in a skillet. **DRAIN.**
HEAT oil in skillet. **PLACE** in 1 tortilla.
FRY tortilla for 15 seconds. **FRY** on other side.
REPEAT with other tortillas. **DRAIN**.
ARRANGE tortillas on a cookie sheet.
SPREAD a thin layer of beans on tortillas.
LAYER beef, then cheese.
BAKE at 350 degrees for 20-30 minutes.
SLICE tortillas into wedges.
SPRINKLE with remaining ingredients.

www.anotherblondemoment.com

Roast Beef Pinwheels
"Kristen Sliced Her Beef!"

1	(8 ounce) cream cheese, softened
1	envelope dry ranch dressing mix
4	10 inch wheat tortillas
8	roast beef deli slices
1	cup lettuce, finely shredded
1	cup shredded Monterey Jack cheese

COMBINE 1st 2 ingredients in a bowl.
SPREAD cream cheese mixture on tortillas.
LAYER next 3 ingredients, in order given.
ROLL into tight logs. **WRAP** in plastic.
CHILL. SLICE. SERVE.

Catalina Pasta Salad
"Richard Catalinaed Cathy"

1	pound ground beef
3/4	cup water
1	envelope dry taco seasoning mix
2	cups shredded cheddar cheese
1	bell pepper, chopped
1	tomato, chopped
1	(4 ounce) can sliced black olives, drained
1	(12 ounce) pasta, cooked according to directions
1	(16 ounce) bottle Catalina dressing

BROWN 1st 3 ingredients in a large skillet. **DRAIN.**
COMBINE all ingredients in a large serving bowl.
COVER. REFRIGERATE for 1 hour.

www.anotherblondemoment.com

Taco Beef Salad
"Not the Same Ole' Beef"

1	**pound ground beef**
1	**envelope dry taco seasoning mix**
³/₄	**cup water**
1	**head of iceberg lettuce, chopped**
2	**cups shredded cheddar cheese**
2	**tomatoes, diced**
1	**bag tortilla chips, crushed**

BROWN 1ˢᵗ 3 ingredients in a skillet. **DRAIN.**
COMBINE all ingredients in a large serving bowl.

DRESSING:
1	**(12 ounce) jar salsa**
1	**(pint) sour cream**

MIX salsa & sour cream in a bowl.
TOSS with beef mixture when ready to serve.

BIMBLABBER - See BIMBABBLE.

Leftover Beef Salad
"McKenzie got Left Over"

1	(12 ounce) bag Romaine lettuce
1/2	cup red onion, chopped
1	bell pepper, chopped
2	tomatoes, chopped
2	cups leftover roast or steak, diced
1	Tablespoon Cavendar's Greek seasoning
1/8	teaspoon pepper
1	Tablespoon olive oil
1/4	cup balsamic vinegar

COMBINE all ingredients in a large serving bowl.
TOSS. SERVE.

Black Bean Beef Soup
"Bubba Browned His Beef"

1	pound ground beef, browned, drained
2	(14 ounce) cans beef broth
2	teaspoons Italian seasoning
1/4	teaspoon onion powder
1/8	teaspoon garlic powder
1	cup elbow macaroni
1	(16 ounce) can diced tomatoes
1	(16 ounce) can black beans

COMBINE 1st 5 ingredients in a large pot.
COOK on medium heat for 10 minutes.
STIR in macaroni. **BOIL** for 2 minutes. **COVER.**
STIR in last 2 ingredients. **BOIL** for 2 minutes.
SIMMER for 30 minutes.

www.anotherblondemoment.com

Cabbage Beef Soup
"A DaVinci Ring"

1	pound ground beef, browned, drained
1	teaspoon garlic salt
1	teaspoon pepper
2	celery stalks, chopped
1	(16 ounce) can kidney beans, drained
½	head cabbage, chopped
1	(28 ounce) can diced tomatoes
1	(28 ounce) can water
4	beef bouillon cubes

COMBINE all ingredients in a large pot.
BOIL for 2 minutes. **COVER.**
SIMMER for 1 hour.

BIMBECILE – An average blonde.

www.anotherblondemoment.com

Hamburger Helper Beef Soup
"An Drew Ashley's Helper"

1	pound ground beef
1	onion, chopped
5	cups water
1	(15 ounce) can whole kernel corn
1	(16 ounce) can diced tomatoes
1	(10 ounce) can Rotel diced tomatoes
2	Tablespoons grated Parmesan cheese
1	Hamburger Helper Lasagna Mix
1	zucchini, sliced, halved

BROWN 1st 2 ingredients in a skillet. **DRAIN.**
COMBINE 1st 6 ingredients in a large pot.
BOIL for 3-5 minutes. **COVER.**
SIMMER for 30 minutes. **STIR** occasionally.
ADD last 3 ingredients. **BOIL** for 2-3 minutes.
COVER. SIMMER for 30 more minutes.

BIMWIT – A blonde with greater than average intelligence for a blonde.

---

www.anotherblondemoment.com

Italian Beef Soup
"Mica or a Wild Italian?"

1	pound ground beef, browned, drained
$1/2$	teaspoon Italian seasoning
6	cups water
1	(6 ounce) box long grain wild rice
2	beef bouillon cubes
$1/2$	teaspoon pepper
2	teaspoons hot sauce
3	cans cream of mushroom soup
1	(4 ounce) can mushroom stems & pieces

COMBINE all ingredients in a large pot.
BOIL for 3-5 minutes. **COVER.**
SIMMER for 1 hour. **STIR** occasionally.

Macaroni Beef Soup
"Rachel Are You Smarter?"

1	pound ground beef, browned, drained
1	quart tomato juice
2	cups water
1	cup elbow macaroni
1	envelope dry onion soup mix
$1/4$	teaspoon chili powder

COMBINE all ingredients in a large pot.
BOIL for 3-5 minutes.
SIMMER for 1 hour. **STIR** occasionally.

www.anotherblondemoment.com

Meatball Soup
"Is His Meat Balled?"

24	ready made frozen meatballs
2	(15 ounce) cans navy beans, rinsed
1	(16 ounce) can diced tomatoes
2	(14 ounce) cans beef broth
1	onion, chopped
2	carrots, sliced
2	zucchinis, sliced
1	teaspoon salt
1	teaspoon pepper

COMBINE all ingredients in a large pot.
BOIL for 3-5 minutes.
SIMMER for 1 hour. **STIR** occasionally.

Vegetable Beef Soup
"Ed Stalked Wanda"

1	pound ground beef, browned, drained
3	cups tomato juice
2	cans condensed beef consommé
2	potatoes, peeled, cubed
2	celery stalks, chopped
2	carrots, grated
1	(10 ounce) bag frozen peas
1	teaspoon sugar
1	(6 ounce) box long grain wild rice

COMBINE all ingredients in a large pot.
BOIL for 3-5 minutes. **SIMMER** for 1 hour.

www.anotherblondemoment.com

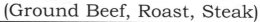

Fajita Beef Stew
"Curt Us Monts"

2	pounds beef stew meat, cubed
1	(14 ounce) can beef broth
2	cups water
1	(16 ounce) frozen fajita style vegetables
1	(14 ounce) can Mexican-style thick & chunky tomato sauce
1	(15 ounce) can pinto beans
2	teaspoons ground cumin
1	(15 ounce) can black beans
	Salt & pepper, to taste

COMBINE all ingredients in a crock-pot.
COOK on **LOW** for 7-8 hours.

BBQ Brisket
"Brisky & Blondequed"

5-6	pound beef brisket
1	envelope dry onion soup mix
1	(10 ounce) bottle Heinz 57 sauce
1	(12 ounce) bottle barbecue sauce
¼	cup Blonde all-purpose seasoning
1	teaspoon pepper

PLACE brisket, cut side up, in a roasting pan.
COMBINE remaining ingredients in a bowl.
POUR over brisket. **COVER.**
BAKE at 350 degrees for 4-5 hours.

www.anotherblondemoment.com

Coca-Cola Brisket
"Danna was Brisky"

5	pound beef brisket
1	(12 ounce) bottle chili sauce
1	envelope dry onion soup mix
2	Tablespoons all-purpose seasoning
1	teaspoon pepper
1	(12 ounce) can coca-cola

PLACE brisket, cut side up, in a roasting pan.
COMBINE remaining ingredients in a bowl.
POUR over brisket. **COVER.**
BAKE at 350 degrees for 4-5 hours.

Crock-Pot Brisket
"Sherry is Mailing"

3	Tablespoons liquid smoke
1	onion, chopped
1	envelope dry onion soup mix
2	Tablespoons dry mustard
2	Tablespoons steak sauce
1	(12 ounce) bottle barbeque sauce
3	Tablespoons Worcestershire
3	Tablespoons all-purpose seasoning
3-4	pound beef brisket

COMBINE all ingredients in a crock-pot.
COOK on **LOW** for 6 hours.

www.anotherblondemoment.com

Rye Bread Brisket
"Rye Brisk Her"

2	onions, chopped
3	slices rye bread, torn into small pieces
4	pound beef brisket
2	garlic cloves, crushed
	Pepper, to taste
1	cup Worcestershire
2	envelopes dry onion soup mix
1	(12 ounce) bottle chili sauce
1	(12 ounce) can beer

ARRANGE onions on the bottom of a roasting pan.
PLACE bread over onions.
PLACE brisket over bread.
RUB brisket with garlic and pepper.
POUR next 4 ingredients over brisket.
BAKE at 350 degrees for 2 hours, **covered**.
REDUCE temperature to 275 degrees.
COOK 2 more hours. **ADD** water as needed.

BIMBABOON - A blonde ancestor.

---

www.anotherblondemoment.com

Italian Meat Loaf
"Carmen is not a Loaf"

1	egg, beaten
2	pounds ground beef
1	cup Italian breadcrumbs
½	onion, chopped
½	bell pepper, chopped
4	cups Italian-style tomato sauce

COMBINE all ingredients in a large bowl.
PLACE in 2 loaf pans.
BAKE at 350 degrees for 1 hour.

Meat Loaf Stuffing
"He Stuffed His Meat"

2	pounds ground beef
1	(6 ounce) box Stove Top Stuffing for beef
⅓	cup ketchup
1	envelope dry onion soup mix
2	eggs, beaten
¾	cup water

COMBINE all ingredients in a large bowl.
PLACE in a loaf pan.
BAKE at 375 degrees for 1 hour.

www.anotherblondemoment.com

Crock-Pot Chuck Roast
"Chuck are You a Crock?"

4-5	**pound chuck roast**
	Olive oil
	Salt & pepper, to taste
	Garlic salt, to taste
	Onion salt, to taste
1	**Reynold's large hot bags**

RUB roast with oil.
RUB all spices into roast with your hand.
PLACE roast in hot bag. **SEAL.**
PLACE roast in hot bag in a crock-pot.
COOK on **HIGH** for 6 hours.

Lemon Pepper Roast
"A Tart Dawn"

$1/4$	**cup lemon pepper**
1	**cup lemon juice**
$1/2$	**cup Worcestershire**
$1/4$	**cup oil**
$1/2$	**cup soy sauce**
3-4	**pound Eye of Round roast**

COMBINE 1st 5 ingredients in a roasting pan.
PLACE roast in marinade for at least 1 hour.
COVER. BAKE at 375 degrees for 2 hours.
TURN oven off. **LEAVE** in oven for 1 hour.

www.anotherblondemoment.com

Horseradish Rib-Eye Steak
"Brooke is Tara at Steak?"

1	(8 ounce) cream cheese, softened
1	cup steak sauce
1	Tablespoon prepared horseradish
2	teaspoons salt
2	teaspoons pepper
4	(4 ounce) rib eye steaks, cut ¾ inch thick

COMBINE 1st 5 ingredients in a saucepan.
HEAT on medium heat until heated all the way.
POUR marinade over steaks.
GRILL until desired doneness. **BASTE**.

BIMMIGRANT - The first blonde to reach this country.

www.anotherblondemoment.com

Brown Sugar Round Steak
"Brown Sugar!"

3	pound round steak, cut 2 inches thick
	Blonde all-purpose seasoning, to taste
1	cup water
¼	cup soy sauce
¼	cup brown sugar
¼	cup lemon juice
1	Tablespoon Worcestershire
1	Tablespoon minced parsley
1	teaspoon hot pepper sauce

SPRINKLE meat generously with seasoning.
COMBINE remaining ingredients in a bowl.
MARINATE in the refrigerator for 2 hours.
GRILL until desired doneness. **BASTE**.

BIMBOSS - Someone who tries to control a group of blondes.

---

www.anotherblondemoment.com

Bean Muffin Beef
"Muffs & Beef"

1	pound ground beef, browned, drained
1	envelope dry chili seasoning mix
1	(8 ounce) can tomato sauce
1	(14 ounce) can kidney beans, rinsed
1	box corn muffin mix
1	cup shredded cheddar cheese

COMBINE 1st 4 ingredients in a bowl.
POUR in a pam-sprayed 9x13 baking dish.
MIX muffin mix according to directions.
POUR batter over meat mixture.
BAKE at 350 degrees for 35-40 minutes
SPRINKLE with cheese.
BAKE for 5 more minutes or until cheese melts.

BIMBASIC - Blonde computer language.

---

www.anotherblondemoment.com

Cajun Corn Bake
"Freddie Baked Bubba"

1	**pound ground beef**
1	**onion, chopped**
6	**slices bacon, cooked drained, crumbled**
1	**can tomato soup**
½	**cup self-rising cornmeal**
2	**eggs, beaten**
2	**cups milk**
1	**(15 ounce) can whole kernel corn**
	Salt & pepper, to taste

BROWN 1st 2 ingredients in a large skillet.
DRAIN. **ADD** next 3 ingredients.
COOK on low heat for 5 minutes.
COMBINE remaining ingredients in a bowl.
SPOON in a pam-sprayed 9x13 baking dish.
BAKE at 325 degrees for 1 hour.

BIMBALD – A result of going to a blonde beautician.

---

www.anotherblondemoment.com

Cheeseburger 'N Fries Bake
"Cheeseburger in Paradise"

2	pounds ground beef, browned, drained
1	can golden mushroom soup
1	can cheddar cheese soup
1	(10 ounce) frozen crinkle-cut French fries
	Salt, to taste
	Pepper, to taste

COMBINE 1st 3 ingredients in a pam-sprayed 9x13 baking dish.
ARRANGE fries over meat mixture.
SPRINKLE with salt & pepper.
BAKE at 350 degrees for 1 hour.

Chili Relano Bake
"A Quick Beef"

1	(9 ounce) can whole green chilies, sliced in half
2	pounds ground beef, browned, drained
4	cups shredded Monterey Jack cheese
3	eggs, beaten
3	cups milk
1	cup Bisquick

PLACE chilies in a pam-sprayed 9x13 dish.
LAYER next 2 ingredients over chilies.
COMBINE last 3 ingredients in a bowl.
POUR over meat mixture.
BAKE at 350 degrees for 45 minutes.

www.anotherblondemoment.com

Chip Layered Beef
"Lay Her Chip"

2	**pounds ground beef**
½	**cup onions, chopped**
1	**(12 ounce) jar chunky salsa**
1	**(15 ounce) can whole kernel corn**
¾	**cup mayonnaise**
1	**Tablespoon chili powder**
1	**teaspoon salt**
2	**cups tortilla chips, crushed**
2	**cups shredded Monterey Jack cheese**

BROWN 1st 2 ingredients in a large skillet.
DRAIN. STIR in next 5 ingredients.
LAYER ½ meat mixture, ½ chips, ½ cheese in a pam-sprayed 9x13 baking dish. **REPEAT**.
BAKE at 350 degrees for 30 minutes.

BIMBUG – A cause of errors in blonde computer programs.

Italian Beef Casserole
"Moore Italian"

2	pounds ground beef
1	onion, chopped
1	bell pepper, chopped
1	envelope dry spaghetti seasoning mix
1	(15 ounce) can tomato sauce
2	cups shredded Mozzarella cheese
1	cup sour cream
1	(8 ounce) can crescent rolls
½	cup grated Parmesan cheese

BROWN 1st 3 ingredients in a large skillet.
DRAIN. STIR in next 2 ingredients.
SIMMER for 5 minutes.
POUR in a pam-sprayed 9x13 baking dish.
MIX next 2 ingredients in a separate bowl.
SPOON on top of beef mixture.
COVER cheese mixture with crescent rolls.
SPRINKLE rolls with Parmesan cheese.
BAKE at 375 degrees for 15-20 minutes.

Mexican Beef Crock-Pot
"A Crock of Mark"

2	pounds ground beef, browned, drained
1	(16 ounce) frozen onions & peppers
1	teaspoon salt
1	pound processed cheese, cubed
2	(15 ounce) cans Mexican stewed tomatoes, reserve liquid
2	(15 ounce) cans whole kernel corn
1	(8 ounce) medium egg noodles, cooked
1	cup shredded cheddar cheese

COMBINE 1st 7 ingredients in a crock-pot.
COOK on **LOW** for 4-5 hours.
ADD noodles. **COOK** 30 more minutes.
SERVE. SPRINKLE with cheese.

BYMNASIUM – An exercise room with blondes in it.

www.anotherblondemoment.com

Mexican Crock-Pot Patties
"Patty Pecked Her Beef"

2	**pounds ground beef**
	Salt & pepper, to taste
1	**(15 ounce) can Mexican-stewed tomatoes**
1	**(6 ounce) box beef-flavored rice mix**
1	**can Mexi-corn, drained**
2	**cups water**

SHAPE beef into small patties.
SPRINKLE with salt & pepper.
PLACE patties in bottom of a crock-pot.
COMBINE remaining ingredients in a bowl.
POUR over beef patties.
COOK on **LOW** for 4-5 hours.

Crock-Pot Pizza
"Crocked or Tossed"

2	**pounds ground beef, browned, drained**
1	**(14 ounce) jar pizza sauce**
1	**(12 ounce) pasta, cooked**
2	**cups shredded Mozzarella cheese**
2	**cups grated Parmesan cheese**
2	**(4 ounce) can stems & pieces mushrooms**
2	**(3 ounce) packages sliced pepperoni**
1/2	**onion, chopped**
1/2	**bell pepper, chopped**

COMBINE all ingredients in a crock-pot.
COOK on **LOW** for 4 hours.

www.anotherblondemoment.com

Potato Beef Bake
"Baked Irish"

4	potatoes, peeled, boiled, mashed
1	(15 ounce) can green beans
2	cans tomato soup
	Salt, to taste
1	pound ground beef, browned, drained
1	cup shredded cheddar cheese

PLACE potatoes in a pam-sprayed 9x13 dish.
HEAT next 4 ingredients in a saucepan.
POUR beef mixture over potatoes.
SPRINKLE with cheese.
BAKE at 350 degrees for 25 minutes.

Pea Pod Fried Rice
"Arkansaucey Fried"

1	red bell pepper, cut into strips
1	(10 ounce) bag frozen pea pods
2	teaspoons oil
3	cups rice, cooked
3	Tablespoons soy sauce
1	pound ground beef, browned, drained

STIR-FRY 1st 3 ingredients in a large skillet.
ADD remaining ingredients. **MIX** well.
PLACE in pam-sprayed 9x13 baking dish.
BAKE at 325 degrees for 15 minutes.

www.anotherblondemoment.com

Zucchini Beef
"Squash His Beef"

2	pounds ground beef
1	onion, chopped
1	Hamburger Helper for lasagna, use sauce mix
5	cups water
1	(15 ounce) can whole kernel corn
1	(16 ounce) can diced tomatoes
1	(10 ounce) can diced Rotel tomatoes
2	Tablespoons grated Parmesan cheese
2	zucchinis, sliced, cut into halves

BROWN 1st 2 ingredients in a large pot. **DRAIN**.
STIR in next 5 ingredients. **HEAT** to boiling.
REDUCE heat. **COVER**. **SIMMER** 15 minutes.
STIR in last 2 ingredients. **COVER**.
COOK 10 more minutes.

BIMBUNGLE- A typical blonde mistake; also referred to as BIMBOTCH, and BIMISTAKE.

---

www.anotherblondemoment.com

How to **'PLUCK'** a Mate

RECIPES for 'INTIMACY'

'INTIMATELY CARING CASSEROLE'

2   **healthy physical relationships**
1   **marinated brain**
2   **very ripe social lives**
6   **chopped prayers a day**

MIX a physical relationship with boundaries.
ADD non-marinated brain for emotional understanding. (That would be the woman's.)
COMBINE physical, emotional, & social skills.
POUR in 6 chopped prayers a day.
BAKE at 90 degrees for entire relationship.

'FRENCH KISS SOUP'

2   **Clean Breaths**
2   **sets of moist lips**
2   **great positions**
4   **Closed Eyes**
0   **Slobber**

BRUSH teeth or suck mints before kissing.
RUN tongue over your lips before kissing.
STAND close together. **TILT** head slightly.
BEFORE lips meet close eyes.
LOWER heat to simmer.
SIMMER on low for 2 hours.
DON'T add last ingredient.

www.anotherblondemoment.com

'INTIMATE' Kissing

Hot and Cold Kiss - Lick your partner's lips so that they're warm, and then gently blow on them.

Mistletoe Kiss - Find mistletoe somewhere and kiss under it.

Letter Kiss - Send your lover a kiss in a love letter by writing the letter X. Then kiss it.

Lick Kiss - Just before kissing, gently run your tongue along you partners lip whether it be the top or bottom.

Lip Sucking Kiss - When kissing gently suck on their lower lip.

Neck Nibble Kiss - Gently nibble up and down your partner's neck.

Nip Kiss - While kissing your partner, nibble on their lips.

Reverse Lips Kiss - It involves standing up and kissing them from over their head. GENTLY draw blood to the surface of the lip by nibbling and sucking.

Kissing the Cavern- Use the lips and tongue to gently tickle and kiss your lover's navel.

Shoulder Kiss - Simply come from behind, embrace and kiss the top of the shoulder.

Sip Kiss - Take a small sip of your favorite drink. Leaving a little bit of it on your lips, kiss your partner.

Talking Kiss - Whisper sweet nothings into the ear.

Teaser Kiss - Starting on the forehead, a sweet short kiss on lips, then move up the arms up to her hand, kiss the hand, then come back up the arm, to her face then kiss the lips.

The Buzzing Kiss - Gently place your lips behind their ear. Gently growl and hum, vibrating your lips and cheeks. Move up and down the neck.

The Whipped Cream Kiss - Dip your finger into some cool whip or whipped cream of your choice. Lick it off slowly, then embrace and kiss them deeply letting their tongue slip over yours for a sweet kiss.

Tiger Kiss - Quietly sneak up behind making sure they do not know what you are going to do. Grab them and gently bite their neck. Make sure to get a few good growls in too.

Trickle Kiss - Take a sip of drink and trickle it slowly into the mouth while kissing.

Virtual Kiss - Send an e-card or a kiss via email with this symbol: :-*

www.anotherblondemoment.com

Chicken Recipes
(Chicken or Turkey)

How to 'PLUCK' a Mate
(RECIPES for 'INTIMACY')

www.anotherblondemoment.com

Chicken Recipes
(Chicken or Turkey)

Chicken Cheese Ball
"A Ranch-Hand Chick"

2	(8 ounce) cream cheese, softened
1	(envelope) dry ranch dressing mix
2	(5 ounce) cans chunk chicken, drained
1	teaspoon salt
1	teaspoon pepper
½	cup pecans, chopped

COMBINE 1ˢᵗ 5 ingredients in a bowl. **MIX** well.
SHAPE into 1 or 2 balls. **REFRIGERATE**.
ROLL in pecans. **WRAP** in plastic wrap.
CHILL 1 hour.
SERVE with crackers.

BIMBALLAD – A song of blonde achievements. (Very short)

Buffalo Chicken Wing Dip
"I Warren You about that Chick"

2	boneless, skinless, chicken breasts
2	(8 ounce) cream cheese, softened
1	(8 ounce) bottle hot sauce
1	cup celery, chopped
	Salt & pepper, to taste
1	cup shredded cheddar cheese

BOIL chicken for 20 minutes. **DRAIN. SHRED.**
MIX all ingredients in a large bowl.
POUR in a pam-sprayed 9x13 baking dish.
BAKE at 350 degrees for 30 minutes.
SERVE with crackers or chips.

BIMINI - An Island of Blondes.

www.anotherblondemoment.com

Chicken Liver Chestnuts
"Live Her Chests!"

10	slices of bacon, cut in half
1	pound chicken livers, cut in quarters
1	(8 ounce) can sliced water chestnuts
1/3	cup soy sauce
2	Tablespoons brown sugar
1	teaspoon ginger

WRAP bacon around chicken liver & chestnut.
SECURE with toothpick. **PLACE** on broiler pan.
COMBINE last 3 ingredients.
BRUSH over chicken liver wrap.
BROIL 15-20 minutes. **TURN. BASTE**.

BIMBRAT - An ill-mannered blonde.

Chicken Cheese Pepper Tarts
"Will You Be Cheesy?"

1	pound ground chicken
1/4	cup bell pepper, chopped
1/2	cup sun-dried tomato pesto
1/2	cup basil pesto
2	cups shredded Mozzarella cheese
24	tart shells, in refrigerated section

COOK chicken until it turns white.
ADD bell pepper to chicken.
STIR in next 3 ingredients.
PLACE tart shells on cookie sheet.
SPOON chicken mixture in tart shells.
BAKE at 350 degrees for 20-25 minutes.

A blonde was filling out an application form for a job. She promptly filled the columns entitled NAME, AGE, ADDRESS, etc. Then she came to the column: SALARY EXPECTED.
She writes, "Yes."

www.anotherblondemoment.com

Italian Chicken Wrappers
"Vince is a Wrapped Chicken"

18	wonton wrappers, in refrigerated section
½	cup bell pepper, chopped
½	cup green onion, chopped
2	teaspoons olive oil
2	boneless, skinless, chicken breasts
⅓	cup mayonnaise
2	Tablespoons Parmesan cheese
½	teaspoon oregano
½	teaspoon basil

PLACE wrappers in pam-sprayed muffin tins.
SAUTÉ next 3 ingredients in a skillet.
BOIL chicken for 20 minutes. **DRAIN. SHRED.**
COMBINE all ingredients in a bowl. **MIX** well.
SPOON 2 Tablespoons of filling into wonton cup.
BAKE at 400 degrees for 5-7 minutes.
SERVE hot.

Artichoke Chicken Salad
"Don't Choke, Chick"

3	boneless, skinless, chicken breasts
1	cup zesty Italian salad dressing
1	(7 ounce) jar marinated artichoke hearts, chopped
1	red bell pepper, chopped
	Salt & pepper, to taste
1	(10 ounce) bag mixed salad greens

BOIL chicken for 20 minutes. **DRAIN. CHOP. COMBINE** 1st 5 ingredients in a large salad bowl. **TOSS** with mixed salad greens.

GAS UP!!!!

A trucker came into a truck stop cafe and placed his order. He said, "I want three flat tires, a pair of headlights and a pair of running boards."

The brand new blonde waitress, not wanting to appear stupid, went to the kitchen and said to the cook, "This guy out there just ordered three flat tires, a pair of headlights and a pair of running boards. What does he think this place is ... an auto parts store?"

"No," the cook said. "Three flat tires mean three pancakes, a pair of headlights is two eggs sunny side up, and running boards are 2 slices of crisp bacon."

"Oh, OK!" said the blonde. She thought about it for a moment and then spooned up a bowl of beans and gave it to the customer.

The trucker asked, "What are the beans for, Blondie?"

She replied, "I thought while you were waiting for the flat tires, headlights and running boards, you might as well gas up!"

---

www.anotherblondemoment.com

Black Bean Chicken Salad
"A Cumin' Chick"

2	boneless, skinless, chicken breasts
1	(15 ounce) can black beans, rinsed, drained

BOIL chicken for 20 minutes. **DRAIN. CHOP.**
COMBINE chicken & beans in a serving bowl.

CUMIN DRESSING:
$3/4$	cup olive oil
$1/4$	cup lemon juice
2	teaspoons Dijon mustard
2	teaspoons cumin

MIX all dressing ingredients in a bowl.
POUR over chicken mixture. **TOSS.**

Debbie & Sherry (both blondes) were IMing each other and Debbie types the upsidedown ! (which is spanish) and Sherry asks, "How did you do that?" Debbie replies, "Easy just turn the keyboard upside down."

www.anotherblondemoment.com

Corkscrew Chicken Salad
"A Corked & Screwed Chick"

3	**boneless, skinless, chicken breasts**
½	**cup bell pepper, chopped**
1	**can cheddar cheese soup**
¼	**cup milk**
1	**cup Picante Sauce**
1	**(12 ounce) package corkscrew pasta, cooked according to directions**

BOIL chicken for 20 minutes. **DRAIN. CHOP.**
COMBINE 1st 5 ingredients in a large pot.
COOK on medium heat for 3-5 minutes.
MIX chicken mixture with pasta.
TOSS on low heat for 5 minutes. **SERVE.**

Q: There were three third-grade girls, a blonde, a brunette, and a redhead. Which one had the best figure?
A: The blonde.... she's 18!

---

www.anotherblondemoment.com

Cracker Chicken Salad
"She's a Cracked Chick"

3	boneless, skinless, chicken breasts
1	can cream of mushroom soup
2	Tablespoons onion, chopped
1	egg, hard-boiled, chopped
1	can cream of chicken soup
½	cup celery, chopped
1	cup mayonnaise
2	cups crackers, crushed, divided, 1 cup
2	Tablespoons margarine, melted

BOIL chicken for 20 minutes. **DRAIN. CHOP.**
MIX 1st 8 ingredients in a large bowl.
POUR in a pam-sprayed 9x13 baking dish.
MIX divided crackers & margarine together.
POUR on top of chicken mixture.
BAKE at 300 degrees for 40-50 minutes.

Q: How did the blonde wreck the helicopter?
A: She got cold and turned off the fan.

---

www.anotherblondemoment.com

Grape Chicken Salad
"Papa Graped Billie"

2	boneless, skinless chicken breasts
1	cup green grapes, halved
1	cup red seedless grapes, halved
1/3	cup celery, chopped
1/2	cup walnuts, chopped
1	cup cucumber ranch dressing

BOIL chicken for 20 minutes. **DRAIN. CHOP.**
COMBINE all ingredients in a serving bowl.
CHILL. SERVE.

Fettuccini Chicken Salad
"Billie's a Dilly Chick"

4	boneless, skinless chicken breasts
1	(12 ounce) bag fettuccini, cooked
3	tomatoes, chopped
1/4	cup capers
1	cup mayonnaise
2	Tablespoons dried dill weed
1	teaspoon salt
1	teaspoon pepper
1	teaspoon Cavendar's Greek seasoning

BOIL chicken for 20 minutes. **DRAIN. CHOP.**
COMBINE all ingredients in a large serving bowl.
COVER. CHILL. SERVE.

www.anotherblondemoment.com

Pineapple Chicken Salad
"A Cinnamon Tree Chick"

2	boneless, skinless chicken breasts
1	(8 ounce) can pineapple chunks
2	Tablespoons Dijon mustard
$\frac{1}{2}$	cup celery, chopped
$\frac{2}{3}$	cup mayonnaise
$\frac{1}{3}$	cup slivered almonds

BOIL chicken for 20 minutes. **DRAIN. CHOP.**
MIX all ingredients in a serving bowl.
CHILL. SERVE.

Vegetable Chicken Salad
"Mary's a Pegged Chick"

2	boneless, skinless chicken breasts
1	(15 ounce) can mixed vegetables
1	(8 ounce) can shoe peg corn
1	bunch green onions, chopped
$\frac{1}{2}$	cup mayonnaise
1	Tablespoon prepared mustard

BOIL chicken for 20 minutes. **DRAIN. CHOP.**
COMBINE all ingredients in a large serving bowl.
MIX well. **CHILL. SERVE.**

www.anotherblondemoment.com

Broccoli Chicken Soup
"Joyce is a Lane Chick"

3	boneless, skinless chicken breasts
1	cup carrots, sliced
1	cup celery, sliced
¼	stick margarine
3	(14 ounce) cans chicken broth
	Salt & pepper, to taste
1	(16 ounce) bag frozen chopped broccoli
2	pounds processed cheese, cubed
3	cans cream of potato soup

BOIL chicken for 20 minutes. **DRAIN. CHOP.**
SAUTÉ 1st 4 ingredients in a large pot.
ADD next 3 ingredients. **BRING** to a boil.
REDUCE heat. **SIMMER** for 30 minutes.
ADD last 2 ingredients. **STIR** occasionally.
SIMMER 15-30 more minutes.

www.anotherblondemoment.com

Chicken Chowder
"Jayne Chicked Austin"

4	boneless, skinless chicken breasts
6	cups water
1	teaspoon salt
1	teaspoon pepper
3	potatoes, peeled, cubed
6	carrots, sliced
1	onion, chopped
1	(10 ounce) bag frozen green peas
1	(13 ounce) can evaporated milk

BOIL chicken for 20 minutes. **DRAIN. CHOP.**
COMBINE 1st 7 ingredients in a large pot.
BRING to a boil. **REDUCE** heat.
SIMMER for 30 minutes.
ADD green peas. **HEAT** for 10 minutes.
STIR in milk. **SIMMER** for 15 more minutes.

Q: Why are there no dumb brunettes?
A: Peroxide.

Chicken Pie Soup
"Robin Pied Berek"

3	boneless, skinless chicken breasts
1	can cream of mushroom soup
3	(14 ounce) cans chicken broth
2	(15 ounce) cans mixed vegetables
	Salt & pepper, to taste
1	(12 ounce) can biscuits, quartered

BOIL chicken for 20 minutes. **DRAIN. SHRED.**
COMBINE 1st 5 ingredients in a large pot.
SIMMER for 30 minutes. **BRING** to a boil.
DROP biscuits into boiling soup mixture.
COVER. SIMMER for 20-30 minutes.

Italian Chicken Soup
"Delana has the Ticket"

2	boneless, skinless chicken breasts
3	(14 ounce) cans chicken broth
1/2	cup rice (not instant)
1	envelope dry onion soup mix
2	envelopes dry Italian dressing mix
1	(28 ounce) can crushed tomatoes

BOIL chicken for 20 minutes. **DRAIN. CHOP.**
COMBINE all ingredients in a large pot.
BRING to a boil. **REDUCE** heat.
SIMMER for 1 hour.

www.anotherblondemoment.com

Mexican Chicken Soup
"Wonderful Things in Georgetown"

4	boneless, skinless chicken breasts
¼	stick margarine
½	onion, chopped
1	can cream of celery soup
1	can cream of mushroom soup
1	can cream of chicken soup
2	(14 ounce) cans chicken broth
2	soup cans of milk
1	(16 ounce) Mexican Velveeta cheese, cubed

BOIL chicken for 20 minutes. **DRAIN. CHOP.**
SET aside.
SAUTÉ next 2 ingredients for 5 minutes.
ADD all ingredients. **COOK** for 10 minutes.
STIR constantly, until cheese melts.

Q: Why don't blondes have elevator jobs?
A: They don't know the route.

---

www.anotherblondemoment.com

Noodle Cheesy Chicken Soup
"A Speckled Hen"

3	boneless, skinless chicken breasts
1	can cheddar cheese soup
4	(14 ounce) cans chicken broth
1	(8 ounce) bag fine egg noodles
1	cup milk
1	cup shredded cheddar cheese

BOIL chicken for 20 minutes. **DRAIN. CHOP.**
COMBINE 1st 5 ingredients in a large pot.
BRING to a boil. **REDUCE** heat.
SIMMER until noodles are soft.
SERVE with cheese.

Taco Chicken Soup
"Dave Chicked Out"

3	boneless, skinless chicken breasts
3	(14 ounce) cans chicken broth
1	onion, chopped
1	(15 ounce) can diced tomatoes
1	(10 ounce) can diced Rotel tomatoes
1	(15 ounce) can black beans
1	(15 ounce) can cream-style corn
1	package dry taco seasoning
1	package dry ranch dressing mix

BOIL chicken for 20 minutes. **DRAIN. CHOP.**
COMBINE all ingredients in a large pot.
SIMMER for 2 hours.

www.anotherblondemoment.com

Rotel Chicken Soup
"A Proctor Breast"

4	boneless, skinless chicken breasts
3	(14 ounce) cans chicken broth
2	(10 ounce) cans diced Rotel tomatoes
1	(16 ounce) can whole kernel corn
1	onion, chopped
1	can tomato soup
1	teaspoon oregano
3	Tablespoons cornstarch
3	Tablespoons water

BOIL chicken for 20 minutes. **DRAIN. CHOP.**
COMBINE 1st 7 ingredients in a large pot.
MIX last 2 ingredients until smooth.
ADD to soup mixture.
BRING to a boil. **REDUCE** heat.
SIMMER for 2 hours.

Q: Why did the blonde hold on to the sandpaper when she was walking through the desert?
A: She thought it was a map.

---

www.anotherblondemoment.com

Vegetable Chicken Soup
"A Mixed Breast Chick"

2	boneless, skinless chicken breasts
3	cups water
1	(8 ounce) can tomato sauce
1	(10 ounce) bag frozen mixed vegetables
1	envelope dry noodle soup mix with real chicken broth
	Salt & pepper, to taste

BOIL chicken for 20 minutes. **DRAIN. CHOP.**
COMBINE all ingredients in a large pot.
BRING to a boil. **SIMMER** for 20 minutes.
STIR. SIMMER for 45 more minutes.

There was a blonde rowing a boat through a wheat field and another blonde was driving by and yelled, "You're the reason they say blondes are stupid". The other blonde says, "Why?" and she said, "Because you're not wearing a life jacket".

---

www.anotherblondemoment.com

BBQ Chicken Bake
"Blondequed Chick"

4	boneless, skinless chicken breasts
1	cup all-purpose flour
4	slices of bacon
1	(8 ounce) can mushroom pieces, drained
2	cups barbecue sauce
	Salt & pepper, to taste

COAT chicken breast in flour.
PLACE chicken in a 9x13 baking dish.
LAY bacon across chicken.
BAKE at 400 degrees for 30 minutes. **DRAIN**.
ADD last 3 ingredients to chicken.
BAKE 10 more minutes.

Q: Why did the blonde bring a gun to the wedding?
A: She was told she was supposed to hold up the bride's train.

---

www.anotherblondemoment.com

BBQ Corn Chip Chicken
"A Corny Chick"

6	boneless, skinless chicken breasts
1	can cream of mushroom soup
1	can cream of chicken soup
2	cups shredded cheddar cheese, divided 1 cup
1	envelope dry taco seasoning
2	cups barbeque corn chips, crushed

PLACE chicken in a pam-sprayed 9x13 dish.
COMBINE next 4 ingredients in a bowl.
POUR soup mixture over chicken.
BAKE at 450 degrees for 30 minutes.
PUT 1 cup cheese & chips over chicken.
BAKE for 5 more minutes.

Q: What do you call two blondes in a cadillac?
A: Duel air bags.

---

www.anotherblondemoment.com

Cheez-it Chicken Bake
"Jim Cheezed that Chick"

1	cup sour cream
1/8	teaspoon salt
1/8	teaspoon pepper
1/8	teaspoon Blonde all-purpose seasoning
4	boneless, skinless chicken breasts
2	cups Cheez-it crackers, crushed

COMBINE 1st 4 ingredients in a bowl.
ROLL chicken in sour cream mixture.
ROLL chicken in crackers.
PLACE chicken in a pam-sprayed 9x13 dish.
BAKE at 325 degrees for 1 hour.

Q: Why did the blonde bring a car door to the desert?
A: She thought it was a map!

---

www.anotherblondemoment.com

Cracker Chicken Bake
"He Cracked that Chick"

2	eggs
2	cups buttery crackers, crushed
½	teaspoon garlic salt
½	teaspoon pepper
4	boneless, skinless chicken breasts
1	stick margarine, sliced

BEAT eggs in a bowl. **SET** aside.
MIX next 3 ingredients in a separate bowl.
DIP chicken in eggs. **COAT** in cracker mixture.
PLACE in a pam-sprayed 9x13 baking dish.
PLACE 2 slices of margarine on each breast.
BAKE at 375 degrees for 40-50 minutes.

Q: A blonde and a scrunchy fell off a cliff. Which landed first?
A: The scrunchy, the blonde had to ask for directions.

---

www.anotherblondemoment.com

Dijon Stuffed Chicken Bake
"Is Angel Stuffed?"

4	boneless, skinless chicken breasts
1	(4 ounce) cream cheese with chives, softened
½	stick margarine, softened, divided
½	cup brown sugar
4	Tablespoons Dijon mustard
	Salt & pepper, to taste

POUND breasts until ¼ inch thick.
CREAM last 5 ingredients in a bowl.
SPREAD mixture on each chicken breast.
FOLD breasts over & **ATTACH** with 2 toothpicks.
MELT remaining margarine & **DRIZZLE** over chicken breast.
PUT chicken in a pam-sprayed 9x13 baking dish.
BAKE at 400 degrees for 35 minutes.

Q: What is the difference between Jupiter and a blondes head?
A: Jupiter isn't hollow.

French Onion Chicken
"Sharon a French Chick"

4	boneless, skinless chicken breasts, browned
2	cans French onion soup
1/2	teaspoon pepper
2	teaspoons Blonde all-purpose seasoning
1	(4 ounce) jar sliced mushrooms, drained
1	cup shredded Mozzarella cheese

COMBINE all ingredients in a crock-pot.
COOK on **LOW** for 5 hours.

Honey Grilled Chicken
"Honey, Who Grilled the Chick?"

2	cups orange juice
1	cup honey
1	envelope dry Italian dressing mix
1/8	teaspoon salt
1/8	teaspoon pepper
6	boneless, skinless chicken breasts

MIX 1st 5 ingredients in a large bowl.
PLACE chicken in mixture.
MARINATE for 1 hour. **TURN.**
PLACE on grill for 25 minutes.
TURN & **BASTE** every 5 minutes.

www.anotherblondemoment.com

Horseradish Grilled Chicken
"Lori Expressed that Chick"

1½	cups chili sauce
¾	cup balsamic vinegar
2	Tablespoons prepared horseradish
2	garlic cloves, crushed
1	teaspoon salt
4	boneless, skinless chicken breasts

COMBINE 1st 5 ingredients in a large bowl.
PLACE chicken in mixture.
MARINATE for 1 hour, **turning** to coat both sides.
PLACE on grill for 25 minutes.
TURN & **BASTE** every 5 minutes.

Lemonade Grilled Chicken
"Christina is a Photo Chick"

3	garlic cloves, crushed
½	stick margarine
⅛	teaspoon salt
⅛	teaspoon pepper
1	(6 ounce) can frozen lemonade, thawed
6	boneless, skinless chicken breasts

SAUTÉ 1st 4 ingredients in a saucepan.
REMOVE from heat. **STIR** in lemonade.
PLACE chicken in mixture.
MARINATE for 1 hour, **turning** to coat both sides.
PLACE on grill for 25 minutes.
TURN & **BASTE** every 5 minutes.

www.anotherblondemoment.com

Peach Chicken Sauté
"Evie Peached Her"

4	boneless, skinless chicken breasts, cubed
1	envelope dry taco seasoning
1	Tablespoon oil
1	(16 ounce) jar chunky salsa
1	(8 ounce) jar peach preserves
¼	cup water

SHAKE 1st 2 ingredients in a zip-lock plastic bag.
BROWN chicken in oil for 5 minutes.
COMBINE last 3 ingredients in a saucepan.
HEAT. STIR until salsa & preserves mix well.
POUR in skillet with chicken.
BRING to a boil. **REDUCE** heat. **COVER**.
SIMMER for 30 minutes. **STIR** occasionally.

Q: What does a blonde do every morning when she looks in the mirror?
A: She introduces herself.

---

www.anotherblondemoment.com

Picante Crock-Pot Chicken
"A Prepared Redhead Chick"

4	boneless, skinless chicken breasts
1	bell pepper, cut into rings
1	(16 ounce) jar picante sauce
½	cup brown sugar
2	Tablespoons prepared mustard
	Salt & pepper, to taste

PLACE 1st 2 ingredients in a crock pot.
STIR remaining ingredients in a separate bowl.
POUR over chicken breasts.
COOK on **LOW** for 5 hours.

Tequila Grilled Chicken
"A Drunk Chick"

¼	cup tequila
1	(6 ounce) can frozen limeade
2	Tablespoons Trip Sec
2	Tablespoons cilantro, chopped
2	garlic cloves, minced
1	jalapeño pepper, seeded, chopped
	Juice of a lime
	Salt & pepper, to taste
4	boneless, skinless chicken breasts

COMBINE 1st 8 ingredients in a large bowl.
PLACE chicken in mixture.
MARINATE for 1 hour. **TURN** to coat both sides.
PLACE on grill for 25 minutes.
TURN & **BASTE** every 5 minutes.

www.anotherblondemoment.com

Vegetable Chicken Sauté
"Ida Weeded Leonard"

3	Tablespoons margarine
4	boneless, skinless chicken breasts
2	cups water
1	envelope dry vegetable soup mix
½	teaspoon dried dill weed
½	cup sour cream

BROWN 1st 2 ingredients in a large skillet.
TURN occasionally.
ADD next 3 ingredients. **BRING** to a boil.
REDUCE heat. **SIMMER** for 30 minutes.
STIR occasionally. **REMOVE** chicken breasts.
STIR in sour cream to skillet mixture.
POUR mixture over chicken breasts.

Q: Did you hear about the two blondes that were found frozen to death in their car at a drive-in movie theater?
A: They went to see "Closed for Winter."

---

www.anotherblondemoment.com

Artichoke Pasta Chicken
"Did that Chick Choke"?

2	**Tablespoons olive oil**
4	**boneless, skinless chicken breasts, cut into strips**
1½	**cups milk**
2	**(4 ounce) jars marinated artichoke hearts**
1	**envelope dry Knorr creamy pesto sauce mix**
1	**(7 ounce) box fettuccini, cooked according to directions**

PLACE olive oil on medium heat in skillet.
ADD chicken strips when oil is hot.
COOK for 6-8 minutes. **TURN** occasionally.
MIX next 3 ingredients in a separate bowl.
ADD artichoke mixture to chicken strips.
SIMMER for 30 minutes. **STIR** occasionally.
POUR over fettuccini. **SERVE.**

Q: Why do blondes put rulers on their foreheads?
A: They want to measure their intelligence.

---

www.anotherblondemoment.com

Asparagus Cheese Chicken
"Oh! Spare Us, Bev"

1	Tablespoon margarine
4	boneless, skinless chicken breasts
1	can broccoli cheese soup
1	(10 ounce) bag frozen asparagus cuts
1/3	cup milk
	Salt & pepper, to taste

BROWN 1st 2 ingredients in a large skillet.
COOK chicken 10-15 minutes on both sides.
REMOVE chicken. **SET** aside.
STIR remaining ingredients in skillet.
RETURN chicken to skillet.
COVER. **SIMMER** for 25 minutes.

Q: Why do blondes stand under light bulbs?
A: It's the closest they'll come to a bright idea.

---

www.anotherblondemoment.com

Biscuit Chicken Bake
"A Baked Chick"

4	boneless, skinless chicken breasts
1	can cream of broccoli soup
1	can cream of potato soup
$\frac{2}{3}$	cup milk
$\frac{1}{2}$	teaspoon poultry seasoning
$\frac{1}{8}$	teaspoon pepper
$\frac{1}{8}$	teaspoon salt
1	(10 ounce) bag frozen mixed vegetables
1	(8 count) can biscuits

BOIL chicken for 20 minutes. **DRAIN. CHOP.**
COMBINE 1st 8 ingredients in a bowl.
POUR in a pam-sprayed 2-quart dish.
BAKE at 400 degrees for 20 minutes. **STIR.**
PLACE biscuits over chicken mixture.
BAKE for 15 more minutes.

Q: Why do blonde nurses bring red magic markers to work?
A: In case they have to draw blood.

Broccoli Chicken Bake
"A Britney Speared Chick"

4	boneless, skinless chicken breasts
1	(16 ounce) bag frozen broccoli spears
2	cans cream of chicken soup
1	cup milk
1/3	cup mayonnaise
2	teaspoons lemon juice
1/2	stick margarine, melted
1	cup bread crumbs
1	cup shredded cheddar cheese

BOIL chicken for 20 minutes. **DRAIN. CHOP.**
BOIL broccoli for 10 minutes.
PLACE broccoli in a pam-sprayed 9x13 dish.
SPRINKLE chicken over broccoli.
COMBINE next 4 ingredients in a saucepan.
HEAT to dilute soup. **POUR** over chicken.
COMBINE last 3 ingredients in a separate bowl.
POUR over chicken.
BAKE at 350 degrees for 30 minutes. **SERVE.**

Q: Did you hear about the blonde who stayed up all night to see where the sun went?
A: It finally dawned on her!

Chicken Pie
"Jacqueline Pied Chel"

2	boneless, skinless chicken breasts
2	cans cream of potato soup
1	(16 ounce) can Veg-All, drained
$\frac{1}{2}$	cup milk
$\frac{1}{2}$	teaspoon thyme
2	9-inch pie crusts

BOIL chicken for 20 minutes. **DRAIN. CHOP.**
COMBINE 1st 5 ingredients in a bowl.
POUR in pie crust.
COVER with other crust. **CRIMP** edges to seal.
BAKE at 375 degrees for 40 minutes.

A REDHEAD'S HUSBAND

A redhead accompanied her husband to the doctor's office. After his checkup, the doctor called the wife into his office alone.

He said, "Your husband is suffering from a very severe disease, combined with horrible stress. If you don't do the following, your husband will surely die. Each morning, fix him a healthy breakfast. Be pleasant, and make sure he is in a good mood. For lunch make him a nutritious meal. For dinner prepare an especially nice meal for him. Don't burden him with chores, as he probably had a hard day. Don't discuss your problems with him, it will only make his stress worse. Most importantly, make love with your husband several times a week and satisfy his every whim. If you can do this for the next 10 months to a year, I think your husband will regain his health completely."

On the way home, the husband asked his wife, "What did the doctor say?"

"You're going to die," she replied.

www.anotherblondemoment.com

Green Bean Chicken Bake
"Phyllis Beaned Lewis"

2	boneless, skinless chicken breasts
1	(10 ounce) bag frozen green beans
1	can cream of chicken soup
1/2	cup mayonnaise
1	teaspoon lemon juice
1/4	teaspoon curry powder
1	cup shredded cheddar cheese
1/3	cup bread crumbs
1/2	stick margarine, melted

BOIL chicken for 20 minutes. **DRAIN. CHOP.**
PLACE beans in a pam-sprayed 9x9 dish.
SPRINKLE chicken over green beans.
COMBINE next 4 ingredients.
POUR over chicken.
COMBINE remaining ingredients in a bowl.
POUR over soup mixture.
BAKE at 350 degrees for 30 minutes.

Macaroni Chicken
"Kimbrell Elbowed Chel"

2	boneless, skinless chicken breasts
3/4	cup milk
1	can cream of chicken soup
1	cup shredded sharp cheddar cheese, divided
1	(4 ounce) can mushroom stems & pieces, drained
1	(2 ounce) jar diced pimientos
	Salt, to taste
	Pepper, to taste
1	cup elbow macaroni, cooked according to directions

BOIL chicken for 20 minutes. **DRAIN. CHOP.**
COMBINE all ingredients in a bowl.
EXCLUDE 1/2 cup cheese.
POUR in a pam-sprayed 9x13 baking dish.
BAKE at 350 degrees for 35 minutes, **covered**.
UNCOVER. **ADD** remaining cheese.
PLACE in oven until cheese melts.

Mexican Chicken Spaghetti
"Memaw is a Noodled Chick"

4	boneless, skinless chicken breasts
1	pound processed cheese, cubed
½	pound Velvetta Mexican cheese, cubed
1	can cream of chicken soup
1	can milk
1	(7 ounce) package spaghetti, cooked according to directions

BOIL chicken for 20 minutes. **DRAIN. CHOP.**
COMBINE 1st 5 ingredients in a large pot.
COOK on low heat until cheese melts.
ADD spaghetti to pot. **TOSS. SERVE.**

Mushroom Chicken Spaghetti
"Make Room for that Chick"

4	boneless, skinless chicken breasts
1	(8 ounce) fresh sliced mushrooms
2	cans cream of chicken soup
1	(7 ounce) spaghetti, cooked according to directions
1	cup shredded cheddar cheese
2	Tablespoons slivered almonds

BOIL chicken for 20 minutes. **DRAIN. CHOP.**
COMBINE all ingredients in a large pot.
HEAT over medium heat for 2-3 minutes.
POUR in a pam-sprayed 2-quart casserole dish.
BAKE at 350 degrees for 30 minutes.

www.anotherblondemoment.com

Parmesan Chicken Pasta
"Busey Baked that Chick"

2	eggs
2	cups Italian bread crumbs
4	boneless, skinless chicken breasts, pounded
½	cup olive oil
1	(8 ounce) can tomato sauce
1	cup Mozzarella cheese

BEAT eggs in a bowl.
POUR bread crumbs in a separate bowl.
DIP chicken in egg, then bread crumbs.
HEAT oil in a large skillet.
BROWN chicken for 15 minutes.
TURN occasionally.
PUT chicken in a pam-sprayed 9x13 dish.
PUT 2 Tablespoons tomato sauce & cheese on each breast.
BAKE at 350 degrees for 25 minutes.
SERVE over pasta.

Q: How many blondes does it take to make a circuit?
A: Two. One to stand in the bathtub, and another to pass her the blow dryer.

---

www.anotherblondemoment.com

Pepperoni Chicken
"Peck & Beck that Ham"

6	boneless, skinless chicken breasts
2	Tablespoons margarine
$\frac{1}{8}$	teaspoon salt
$\frac{1}{8}$	teaspoon pepper
24	pepperoni slices
6	Mozzarella cheese slices

BROWN 1st 4 ingredients in a large skillet.
PLACE chicken in a pam-sprayed 9x13 dish.
PLACE 4 pepperoni on each piece of chicken,
BAKE at 350 degrees for 25 minutes.
TOP each chicken breast with a Mozzarella slice.
BAKE for 5 more minutes.

Q: What do you call 4 Blondes in a Volkswagon?
A: Far-from-thinkin.

---

www.anotherblondemoment.com

Potato BBQ Chicken
"Blondequed Barbie Chick"

4	**boneless, skinless chicken breasts**
1	**(12 ounce) bottle barbecue sauce**
3	**baking potatoes, peeled, sliced thin**
1	**green bell pepper, sliced thin**
1	**red bell pepper, sliced thin**
1	**onion, sliced**

TEAR two sheets of foil the length of a cookie sheet.

PLACE one sheet on the bottom of the cookie sheet.

SPOON half the barbecue sauce in the center of the cookie sheet.

PLACE the chicken on top of the sauce.

LAYER potatoes, peppers & onions on top.

POUR the remaining barbecue sauce over onions.

PLACE the other sheet of foil on top.

FOLD the edges together.

BAKE at 350 degrees for 50-60 minutes.

Q: Did you hear about the blonde skydiver?
A: She missed the Earth!

---

www.anotherblondemoment.com

Sweet Potato Chicken
"Lemuria Chick"

½	cup flour, plus 2 Tablespoons
½	teaspoon ground nutmeg
½	teaspoon cinnamon
4	boneless, skinless chicken breasts
3	sweet potatoes, peeled, sliced
½	cup brown sugar
1	(10 ounce) can cream of chicken soup
1	cup orange juice
1	teaspoon vanilla

COMBINE 1st 3 ingredients in a bowl. **SET** aside.
COAT chicken in flour mixture.
PLACE sweet potatoes in a crock-pot.
PLACE chicken on potatoes.
COMBINE last 4 ingredients in a bowl.
POUR over chicken.
COOK on **MEDIUM** for 4 hours.

Q: How can you tell when a blonde rejects a new brain transplant?
A: She sneezes.

---

www.anotherblondemoment.com

Brown Rice Chicken Bake
"Ti Browned that Chick"

1	cup Italian dressing
1	Tablespoon Blonde all-purpose seasoning
4	boneless, skinless chicken breasts
2	cups brown rice, cooked according to directions
1	can fiesta nacho cheese soup
1	(10 ounce) can diced Rotel tomatoes

MIX 1st 2 ingredients in a large bowl.
PLACE chicken in mixture.
MARINATE. TURN to coat both sides.
PLACE on grill for 25 minutes.
TURN & **BASTE** every 5 minutes
CUT chicken into strips
COMBINE remaining ingredients in a bowl.
ADD chicken to rice mixture.
SPOON in a pam-sprayed 2-quart casserole dish.
BAKE at 350 degrees for 20 minutes, **covered**.

Q: How can you tell if a blonde writes mysteries?
A: If she has a checkbook.

---

www.anotherblondemoment.com

Yellow Rice Chicken
"A Yellow-Bellied Chick"

8	boneless, skinless chicken breasts
1	(15 ounce) can Mexican-stewed tomatoes
1½	cups long grain rice, uncooked
1	(5 ounce) package yellow rice seasoning mix
2	(14 ounce) cans chicken broth
1	garlic clove, crushed
1	teaspoon oregano
1	teaspoon chili powder
1	cup water

COMBINE all ingredients in a crock-pot.
COOK on **LOW** for 7-8 hours.

Q: How can you tell if a blonde is a good cook?
A: She gets the pop-tarts out of the toaster in one piece.

---

www.anotherblondemoment.com

Spinach Spaghetti Chicken
"Ronnie's Inside Story"

1	(10 ounce) bag frozen chopped spinach
1	can cream of chicken soup
3/4	cup of mayonnaise
2	Tablespoons lemon juice
1	(7 ounce) package spaghetti, cooked according to directions
4	boneless, skinless chicken breasts

PUT spinach in a pam-sprayed 9x13 baking dish.
COMBINE next 4 ingredients in a bowl.
POUR spaghetti mixture over spinach.
PLACE chicken on top of spaghetti mixture.
COVER. **BAKE** at 350 degrees for 1 hour.

Q: Why did the blonde get fired from the banana plantation?
A: Because she threw out all the bent ones.

---

www.anotherblondemoment.com

Swiss Cheese Chicken
"Whiney Chick"

6	boneless, skinless chicken breasts
6	Swiss cheese slices
1	can cream of chicken soup
½	cup white wine
2	cups Pepperidge Farm herb stuffing
1	stick margarine, melted

PUT chicken in a pam-sprayed 9x13 baking dish.
PUT a cheese slice on each piece of chicken.
COMBINE next 2 ingredients in a bowl.
POUR over chicken.
PLACE stuffing over chicken.
POUR margarine over chicken.
BAKE at 350 degrees for 50-60 minutes.

Q: How do you get a blonde to stay in the shower all day?
A: Give her a bottle of shampoo that says "Lather, rinse, repeat."

---

www.anotherblondemoment.com

How to 'BORE' a Mate

RECIPES for 'BREAKING UP'

'Honey-Do Linguini'

1	realization of problem
2	acknowledgements of problem
1	week without talking
2	good friends
	a splash of forgiveness

POUR acknowledgement & realization of problems in a large bowl. **MIX** well.
ADD 1 week without communicating.
BRING friends into your life for support.
POUR forgiveness into colander.
DRAIN all anger & guilt.
DON'T look for a rebound.

Q: What was the blonde psychic's greatest achievement?
A: An IN-body experience!

---

www.anotherblondemoment.com

RECIPES for 'BREAKING UP'

'Breaking Up Brownies'

1   cup of caring
1   cup of wanting
2   cups of guilt-free emotions
3   cups of not taking it personal
1   Tablespoon of no telling
1   gallon memories
     a splash of fresh start

UNDERSTANDING caring for a person
& **wanting** a person is 2 different emotions.
POUR guilty feelings in the garbage.
DISPOSE of the hurt feelings.
POUR in 1 Tablespoon of not telling
secrets of the relationship.
STIR in the gallon of memories & be
done with the relationship.
BAKE at 350 degrees for a fresh start.

YIELD: ANGER MANAGEMENT CLASSES may
be needed if either party can't get over it.

Remember... **Smart Blondes have dark roots!**

www.anotherblondemoment.com

Pork Recipes

(Bacon, Ham, Pepperoni, Pork Chops, Ribs, Roast, Salami, Sausage, Steak)

How to 'BORE' a Mate

(RECIPES for 'BREAKING UP')

www.anotherblondemoment.com

Pork Recipes
(Bacon, Ham, Pepperoni, Pork Chops, Ribs, Roast, Salami, Sausage, Steak)

6 Layer BBQ Bacon
"Lay Her Blondequed"

2	(8 ounce) cream cheese, softened
1	cup barbecue sauce
2	(3 ounce) bags real bacon pieces
2	tomatoes, chopped
1	bunch green onions, chopped
3	cups shredded cheddar cheese

SPREAD cream cheese on pizza pan.
TOP with barbecue sauce.
SPRINKLE remaining ingredients, in order.
BAKE at 350 degrees for 15 minutes.
SERVE with crackers.

Bacon Cheese Log
"Harp Her Laws"

1	(8 ounce) cream cheese, softened
½	cup pecans, chopped
¼	teaspoon garlic salt
¼	teaspoon Worcestershire
4	drops of hot sauce
1	pound bacon, cooked, drained, crumbled

MIX all ingredients in a bowl.
SHAPE into a log roll.
WRAP tightly in wax paper. **CHILL**.
SERVE with crackers.

www.anotherblondemoment.com

Bacon Cheese Spread
"Streaky Rasher Spread"

1	round loaf of sourdough bread
1	(8 ounce) cream cheese, softened
2	cups sour cream
2	cups shredded cheddar cheese
2	teaspoons Worcestershire
2	(3 ounce) bags real bacon pieces

CUT top off bread. **HOLLOW** out inside.
COMBINE remaining ingredients in a bowl.
SPOON into dough. **WRAP** in foil.
BAKE at 325 degrees for 50-60 minutes.
SERVE with crackers.

Bacon Spinach Balls
"New Leaf Flitch"

1	(3 ounce) bag real bacon pieces
2	eggs, beaten
1	(10 ounce) bag chopped spinach, thawed, drained
1	cup seasoned croutons, crushed
1/2	cup parmesan cheese
2	Tablespoons margarine, softened

COMBINE all ingredients in a bowl. **MIX** well.
SHAPE into marble-size balls.
PLACE on ungreased cookie sheet.
BAKE at 350 degrees for 15 minutes.

www.anotherblondemoment.com

Bacon Swiss Pleasers
"Eye Am Pleasing You"

1	**(8 ounce) can crescent rolls**
6	**Swiss cheese slices**
3	**eggs, beaten**
¾	**cup milk**
1	**Tablespoon minced onions**
8	**bacon slices, cooked, drained, crumbled**

PRESS rolls in pam-sprayed 9x13 baking dish.
PLACE cheese slices on dough.
COMBINE remaining ingredients in a bowl.
POUR in dish.
BAKE at 425 degrees for 15 minutes.
CUT into 2-inch squares.

Blue Cheese Bacon Dip
"A Bell of the Ball"

1	**cup sour cream**
1	**(8 ounce) cream cheese, softened**
1	**cup crumbled blue cheese**
1	**Tablespoon minced onion**
1	**(3 ounce) bag real bacon pieces**
1	**bell pepper, top & inside hollowed out**

COMBINE 1st 5 ingredients in a bowl. **CHILL**.
SPOON mixture into hollowed-out bell pepper.
SERVE with vegetables or crackers.

www.anotherblondemoment.com

Cheddar Ham Wafers
"Swayze Crazie Wafers"

½	cup ground ham
1	stick margarine, softened
2	cups shredded sharp cheddar cheese
⅓	cup grated Parmesan cheese
½	teaspoon paprika
¼	teaspoon salt
¼	teaspoon pepper
4	drops of hot sauce
1½	cups self-rising flour

COMBINE all ingredients in a bowl. **MIX** well.
FORM into 1-inch balls.
PRESS balls down with a fork.
BAKE at 350 degrees for 15 minutes.

Dijon Ham Scoops
"WE WE Scoops"

1	cup cooked ham, finely chopped
1	stick margarine, softened
2	teaspoons Dijon mustard
2	teaspoons Worcestershire
	Fritos Scoops corn chips
½	cup sliced green olives

COMBINE 1st 4 ingredients in a bowl. **MIX** well.
PLACE a teaspoon of ham into each chip.
TOP each chip with a green olive slice.

www.anotherblondemoment.com

Ham & Cheese Ball
"Frawley is Haming it Up"

1	(8 ounce) cream cheese, softened
¼	cup mayonnaise
1	cup cooked ham, finely chopped
4	Tablespoons parsley, divided
¼	teaspoon dry mustard
1	Tablespoon green onions, chopped

COMBINE all ingredients in a bowl.
FORM into a ball.
CHILL. **ROLL** ball in 2 Tablespoons parsley.
SERVE with crackers.

Ham & Cheese Log
"Hammered & Logged"

1	cup shredded cheddar cheese
1	stick margarine, softened
½	cup green onions, chopped
2	(8 ounce) cream cheese, softened
1	cup cooked ham, finely chopped
1	Tablespoon Worcestershire

COMBINE all ingredients in a bowl.
FORM into 1 or 2 logs. **CHILL**.
SERVE with crackers.

www.anotherblondemoment.com

Ham Horseradish Bites
"A Condimented Bite"

1	cup cooked ham, chopped
½	cup shredded cheddar cheese
3	Tablespoons mayonnaise
2	Tablespoons margarine, melted
1	Tablespoon prepared mustard
1	teaspoon cream-style horseradish
⅛	teaspoon salt
25	(2-inch) crackers
25	pickle slices

COMBINE 1st 7 ingredients in a bowl. **MIX** well.
SPREAD ham mixture on crackers.
TOP each cracker with a pickle slice. **BROIL**.

Olive Ham Rolls
"Olivia with Chelly Rolls"

1	(3 ounce) cream cheese, softened
1	Tablespoon steak sauce
1	Tablespoon onion, finely chopped
4	drops of hot sauce
6	slices cooked ham, 1/8 inch thick
30	stuffed green olives

COMBINE 1st 4 ingredients in a bowl. **MIX** well.
SPREAD mixture on ham.
PLACE olive near edge of each ham slice.
ROLL up like a jelly roll. **CUT** into 6 slices.
CHILL. **SPEAR** with toothpick.

www.anotherblondemoment.com

Pepperoni Sticks
"Stick it Up Vince"

24	large mushrooms, washed, stems removed
1/2	stick margarine, melted
3	hot pepperoni sticks, thinly sliced
1/2	cup shredded cheddar cheese
1/2	cup shredded Mozzarella cheese
1/2	cup shredded Colby cheese

PLACE caps, rounded side up, in large broiler pan.
BRUSH with butter. **BROIL** for 1 minute.
TURN mushrooms over.
PLACE pepperoni slice in each mushroom.
TOP with shredded cheeses.
BROIL until cheese melts. **SERVE** warm.

Salami Wedges
"Christy is Cured"

1	(3 ounce) cream cheese, softened
2	Tablespoons mayonnaise
2	teaspoons chopped chives
3	dashes of hot sauce
1/8	teaspoon salt
25	thin slices of salami

MIX 1st 5 ingredients in a bowl.
MAKE 5 stacks of salami slices.
SPREAD cheese mixture between slices. **CHILL**.
CUT each stack into 6 equal wedges.

www.anotherblondemoment.com

Bacon Breakfast Casserole
"Lowell is Bacon for a Fast Break"

2	cans cream of mushroom soup
2	cups milk
	Salt & pepper, to taste
8	eggs, hard-boiled, peeled, chopped
1	pound turkey bacon, cooked, chopped
1	cup shredded cheddar cheese

COMBINE 1st 3 ingredients in a bowl. **MIX** well.
POUR in pam-sprayed 9x13 baking dish.
FOLD eggs & bacon in mixture.
BAKE at 350 degrees for 20 minutes.
SPRINKLE with cheese. **MELT** cheese.

Bacon Tomato Cups
"Pegging a Full Cup"

8	slices of turkey bacon, cooked, chopped
1	medium tomato, chopped
½	cup onion, chopped
1	cup shredded Swiss cheese
½	cup mayonnaise
1	(10 ounce) can flaky biscuits

COMBINE 1st 5 ingredients in a bowl. **MIX** well.
SEPARATE each biscuit into 3 thinner biscuits.
PLACE layers in pam-sprayed muffin tins.
FILL biscuits cups with bacon mixture.
BAKE at 375 degrees for 10-12 minutes.

www.anotherblondemoment.com

Canadian Bacon Poached Egg Bake
"My Canadian Friends"

12	Canadian bacon slices
1½	cup shredded Swiss cheese
12	eggs
1	cup whipping cream
½	cup Parmesan cheese
	Salt & pepper, to taste

LAYER 1st 2 ingredients in pam-sprayed 9x13 baking dish.
CRACK eggs (DON'T break yolk).
PLACE each egg on cheese & Canadian bacon.
POUR cream over eggs.
BAKE at 450 degrees for 10 minutes.
SPRINKLE with last 3 ingredients.
BAKE for 8-10 more minutes.
LET stand for 5 minutes before serving.

Q: Why did the blonde pee on the floor?
A: Because the sign said "Wet Floor"!

Canadian Bacon Spinach
"Park Her Paige"

3/4	cup sliced fresh mushrooms
2	Tablespoons onions, chopped
1	teaspoon margarine
4	eggs, beaten
1/4	cup milk
6	slices Canadian bacon, 1/4 inch pieces
1	cup shredded sharp cheddar cheese
2	cups fresh baby spinach leaves, washed
2	Tablespoons tomatoes, chopped

SAUTÉ 1st 3 ingredients for 5 minutes.
ADD next 4 ingredients, **STIR** occasionally.
PLACE 1/2 cup spinach on salad plate.
TOP each spinach leaf with egg mixture.
SPRINKLE with tomatoes.

Q: How did the blonde kill her toy poodle?
A: Trying to put batteries in it.

---

www.anotherblondemoment.com

Ham & Cheese Grits Bake
"Grit Your Teeth!"

3½	cups milk, divided 1½ cups, 2 cups
2¼	cups water
1¼	cups quick-cooking grits
¾	cup cooked ham, diced
1	cup shredded Monterey Jack cheese
2	Tablespoons grated Parmesan cheese
¼	(4 ounce) can chopped jalapeños
2	eggs, beaten
3	egg whites, beaten

COMBINE 1st 2 ingredients in a saucepan.
BRING to a boil over medium heat.
STIR in grits. **REDUCE** heat to low.
SIMMER for 5 minutes, **covered.**
STIR occasionally.
REMOVE from heat.
STIR in next 4 ingredients.
WHISK egg, egg whites and 2 cups milk in a large bowl.
COMBINE all ingredients. (Mixture is lumpy).
POUR in pam-sprayed 2-quart casserole dish.
BAKE at 325 degrees for 45-50 minutes.
LET stand for 10 minutes before serving.

Link Sausage Pancakes
"Link to the Bird Barn"

1	cup pancake mix
1	egg, beaten
1	Tablespoon oil
1	cup milk
1/8	teaspoon vanilla
9	pork sausage links, cooked, drained, cut 1/4 inch thick

COMBINE 1st 5 ingredients in a bowl. **MIX** well.
POUR batter in pam-sprayed 9x9 baking dish.
SCATTER sausage slices over batter.
BAKE at 450 degrees for 20-25 minutes.

Sausage Burritos
"Roll & Tuck Ellen"

6	large flour tortillas
1/2	pound ground sausage, cooked, drained
5	eggs, beaten
2	Tablespoons milk
2/3	cup shredded cheddar cheese
	Salsa

WRAP tortillas tightly in foil.
BAKE at 250 degrees for 15 minutes.
STIR next 3 ingredients into a skillet.
REMOVE when eggs are slightly moist.
SPOON mixture into middle of tortillas.
TOP with cheese & 1 Tablespoon of salsa.
ROLL up. **TUCK** ends inside the rolls.

www.anotherblondemoment.com

Sausage Cheddar Bake
"Quick & Hot"

1	**pound hot sausage, cooked, crumbled**
1	**cup shredded cheddar cheese**
1	**cup Bisquick**
5	**eggs, beaten**
2	**cups milk**
1/8	**teaspoon salt**

PUT sausage in a pam-sprayed 9x13 baking dish.
SPRINKLE with cheese.
COMBINE remaining ingredients in a bowl.
POUR over cheese.
BAKE at 350 degrees for 35 minutes, **covered.**

Q: A bleached blonde and a natural blonde were on top of the Empire State Building. How do you tell them apart?
A: The bleached blonde would never throw bread to the helicopters.

---

www.anotherblondemoment.com

Sausage Pepper Bake
"Barbara is a Hannon"

1	pound sausage
½	bell pepper, chopped
1	(10 ounce) can diced Rotel tomatoes
½	cup hot chunky salsa
1	(8 ounce) processed cheese, cubed
10	eggs, beaten
1	teaspoon salt
½	cup sour cream
⅔	cup milk

BROWN 1st 2 ingredients in a skillet. **DRAIN**.
COMBINE next 3 ingredients with sausage.
COOK until cheese melts.
MIX remaining ingredients in a bowl.
POUR in a pam-sprayed 9x13 baking dish.
BAKE at 325 degrees for 25 minutes.

Q: Did you hear about the new epidemic among blondes?
A: It's called MAIDS - if they don't get one, they die.

---

www.anotherblondemoment.com

Bacon Pesto Pasta Salad
"Angela Rehabs Pesto"

1	(12 ounce) pasta, cooked according to directions
1	pound turkey bacon, cooked, crumbled
1	(8 ounce) Mozzarella cheese, $\frac{1}{4}$ inch cubes
1	(14 ounce) jar roasted sweet red peppers, drained, chopped
	Salt & pepper, to taste
1	(7 ounce) jar basil pesto sauce

COMBINE 1st 5 ingredients in a large bowl.
TOSS pesto with pasta when ready to serve.

Bacon Spinach Salad
"Green is Susan"

2	(9 ounce) bags fresh spinach, washed, dried
1	(12 ounce) bottle spinach salad dressing
1	pound turkey bacon, cooked, chopped
1	(15 ounce) can mandarin oranges, drained
	Cavendar's Greek seasoning, to taste
	Pepper, to taste

COMBINE all ingredients in a large serving bowl.

www.anotherblondemoment.com

Artichoke Ham Pasta Salad
"Linda is a Chokin' Logan"

2	Tablespoons olive oil
1/2	cup red onion, slivered
1	bell pepper, cut into strips
2	cups ham, cut into cubes
1	small jar marinated artichoke hearts
1	(4 ounce) can sliced black olives
1/4	cup dry white wine
1	cup basil leaves
1	(12 ounce) penne pasta, cooked according to directions

SAUTÉ 1st 3 ingredients in large saucepan.
STIR in next 5 ingredients.
COOK until ham pieces are warm.
POUR over pasta. **TOSS.**

Q: Why did the blonde call the welfare office?
A: She wanted to know how to cook food stamps!

---

www.anotherblondemoment.com

Iceberg Ham Salad
"She is Cold as Ice"

2	cups cooked ham, diced
2	cups cooked turkey, diced
2	cups shredded Mozzarella cheese
1	small red onion, chopped
1	(4 ounce) can sliced black olives, drained
1	tomato, chopped
1	head of iceberg lettuce, chopped
1/3	cup balsamic vinegar
2	Tablespoons olive oil

COMBINE all ingredients in a large serving bowl.
TOSS. **SERVE.**

Macaroni Ham Salad
"Is this a Faux Pas, Betty?"

1	(12 ounce) macaroni, cooked according to directions
1	cup cooked ham, cut in strips
1	(8 ounce) processed cheese, cut in strips
1	(8 ounce) can pineapple tidbits, drained
1/2	cup chopped sweet pickles
1	cup celery, sliced
1	teaspoon minced onions
1	(2 ounce) jar diced pimientos
1	cup Southwestern Ranch dressing

COMBINE all ingredients in a bowl. **MIX** well.
CHILL. **SERVE.**

www.anotherblondemoment.com

Potato Ham Dill Salad
"Gary Quartered Kim"

6	potatoes, peeled, cut into 1-inch slices
4	cups water
2	Tablespoons capers
1	Tablespoon dried dill weed
1	(14 ounce) can artichoke hearts
1	cup cooked ham, chopped
3	Tablespoons mayonnaise
1	teaspoon Dijon mustard
	Salt, to taste

BOIL 1st 2 ingredients for 12 minutes. **DRAIN.**
COMBINE all ingredients in a large serving bowl.

Potato Ham Durkee Salad
"Tossed & Durked"

2	cups ham, cooked, diced
8	bacon slices, cooked, crumbled
12	new potatoes, cooked, cut in quarters
3	hard-boiled eggs, chopped
½	cup mayonnaise
½	cup Durkees's dressing

COMBINE all ingredients in a large serving bowl.
TOSS to coat. **SERVE.**

www.anotherblondemoment.com

Bacon Potato Soup
"Did Dakota Get Canned?"

5	potatoes, peeled, cooked, diced
4	cans cheddar cheese soup
2	cans cream of celery soup
3	soup cans of milk
1	pound bacon, cooked, crumbled
1	bunch green onions, chopped

COMBINE all ingredients in a large pot.
BOIL for 2 minutes. **SIMMER** for 55 minutes.

Ham Black Bean Soup
"Is it Cumin?"

2	(15 ounce) cans black beans
2	cups ham, diced
3	jalapeños, seeded, chopped
2	(14 ounce) cans chicken broth
4	cups water
2	teaspoons cumin
$\frac{1}{2}$	teaspoon oregano
1	teaspoon chili powder
$\frac{1}{8}$	teaspoon cayenne pepper

COMBINE all ingredients in a large pot.
BOIL for 2 minutes.
SIMMER for 50 minutes. **SERVE.**

www.anotherblondemoment.com

Leftover BBQ Pork Soup
"Not Sloppy Seconds"

1	quart milk
2	(14 ounce) cans chicken broth
4	cups leftover BBQ pulled pork
1	bunch green onions, chopped
3	drops of hot sauce
2	teaspoons Worcestershire

COMBINE all ingredients in a large pot.
BOIL for 2 minutes. **SIMMER** for 1 hour.

Cajun Corn & Sausage Soup
"Corny & Stued"

1	cup onion, chopped
1	cup bell pepper, chopped
2	teaspoons oil
3	(14 ounce) cans chicken broth
2	(14 ounce) cans Cajun-style stewed tomatoes
1	(6 ounce) can tomato paste
2	(10 ounce) frozen whole kernel corn
2	(pounds) smoked sausage, cooked sliced
4	drops of hot sauce

SAUTÉ 1st 3 ingredients in a skillet.
COMBINE all ingredients in a large pot.
BOIL for 2 minutes. **SIMMER** for 1 hour.

www.anotherblondemoment.com

Peachy Glazed Ham
"Michelle Glazed Her Hams"

1	(15 ounce) can sliced peaches, reserve $\frac{1}{2}$ cup syrup
2	Tablespoons brown sugar
2	teaspoons Dijon mustard
1	pound center-cut ham slice
$\frac{1}{3}$	cup green onions, chopped
$\frac{1}{8}$	teaspoon pepper

COMBINE reserved peach syrup & next 2 ingredients in a large skillet.
COOK over medium heat for 5 minutes.
ADD ham. **COOK** on each side for 5 minutes.
ADD peaches & last 2 ingredients.
COOK on low for 5 minutes.
SERVE.

Q: What do you call it when a blonde gets taken over by a demon?
A: A vacant possession.

---

www.anotherblondemoment.com

Blue Cheese Pork Chops
"Jay Porked Her"

2	Tablespoons margarine
4	thick cut pork chops
1/2	teaspoon pepper
1/2	teaspoon garlic powder
1	cup whipping cream
2	ounces blue cheese, crumbled

MELT margarine in a large skillet.
SEASON chops with next 2 ingredients.
FRY chops in butter about 20-25 minutes.
TURN occasionally. **REMOVE** chops to a plate.
STIR the remaining ingredients in skillet.
COOK, stirring constantly until sauce thickens.
POUR sauce over pork chops.

Q: What two things are necessary to keep a redhead happy?
A: One is to let her think she is having her way and the other is to let her have it.

---

www.anotherblondemoment.com

Cranberry Pork Chops
"French Kiss Chops"

1	cup flour
1	Tablespoon oil
4	pork chops
1	(8 ounce) bottle French dressing
1	(15 ounce) can whole cranberries
1	envelope dry onion soup mix

COAT chops with flour. **FRY** in hot oil.
PLACE chops on foil in 9x13 baking dish.
COMBINE remaining ingredients in a bowl.
POUR over chops.
BAKE at 350 degrees for 1$\frac{1}{2}$ hours.

Q: What can a blonde do if she falls from a boat, in order not to drown?
A: Close her mouth and put her fingers in her ears. She will stay floating until the help arrives.

---

www.anotherblondemoment.com

Lemon Pepper Caper Pork
"Pickled Pork"

2	teaspoons lemon pepper
2	teaspoons Cavendar's Greek seasoning
6	boneless pork tenderloin chops, thinly sliced
1	cup flour
2	teaspoons margarine
¼	cup white wine
¼	cup lemon juice
¼	cup lime juice
¼	cup capers

SPRINKLE pork with 1st 2 ingredients.
COAT pork in flour. **MELT** margarine in skillet.
COOK pork over medium heat for 5-8 minutes on each side.
ADD next 3 ingredients.
COOK sauce until thicken.
SPRINKLE with capers.

Q: Why do some of blondes drown even if they do close their mouths and ears?
A: Because for some of them the volume of their heads is too small to keep them floating.

---

www.anotherblondemoment.com

Sour Cream Pork Chops
"Cream His Chops"

3	Tablespoons margarine
1	onion, chopped
1	garlic clove, chopped
6	pork chops
	Salt & pepper, to taste
1	(14 ounce) can chicken broth
1	bay leaf
1	cup sour cream
2	teaspoons paprika

SAUTÉ 1st 3 ingredients in a large skillet.
SPRINKLE chops with salt & pepper.
BROWN chops in skillet.
ADD next 2 ingredients.
SIMMER for 1 hour, **covered.**
PLACE chops on a serving plate.
HEAT remaining ingredients & garlic mixture.
POUR over pork chops.

Q: How can you tell a blonde with a runny nose from a healthy blonde, without looking at their faces?
A: Knock on their heads - the one with the perfect hollow sound is healthy.

---

www.anotherblondemoment.com

Soy Sauce Pork Chops
"Ferment Her Chops"

1	cup soy sauce
2	Tablespoons balsamic vinegar
2	teaspoons honey
2	teaspoons garlic powder
1	teaspoon pepper
4	pork chops

COMBINE 1st 5 ingredients in a shallow dish.
PLACE chops in sauce. **MARINATE** for 2 hours.
BASTE with marinade occasionally.
GRILL until desired doneness.

Crock-Pot Pork Ribs
"Ribbing to Pork Her"

4	pounds boneless pork spareribs
	Salt & pepper, to taste
1	cup chili sauce
1	cup brown sugar
$\frac{1}{2}$	cup water
2	Tablespoons Worcestershire

SPRINKLE ribs with salt & pepper.
PLACE ribs in crock-pot.
MIX remaining ingredients in a bowl.
POUR over ribs.
COOK on **LOW** for 5-6 hours.

www.anotherblondemoment.com

Sauerkraut Boston Butt Roast
"Roast Her Fermented Butt"

3	pound Boston Butt pork roast
1	cup brown sugar
1	envelope dry onion soup mix
1/8	teaspoon pepper
1/8	teaspoon salt
2	(15 ounce) cans of sauerkraut

PLACE roast in crock-pot.
MIX remaining ingredients in a large bowl.
POUR over roast. **COOK** on **HIGH** for 1 hour.
COOK on **LOW** for 6-8 hours.

Taco Pork Roast
"Shoulder Landon"

4	pound pork shoulder roast
2	(4 ounce) cans diced green chilies
1/4	cup chili powder
1	teaspoon dried oregano
1	envelope dry taco seasoning
2	teaspoons minced garlic

PLACE roast on foil.
COMBINE remaining ingredients in a bowl.
RUB mixture all over roast.
WRAP foil completely around roast.
PLACE roast on top of a roasting rack.
BAKE at 300 degrees for 4 hours.

www.anotherblondemoment.com

Dijon Pork Steaks
"Bev Porked Her Mark"

6	garlic cloves, chopped
2	Tablespoons soy sauce
2	Tablespoons Dijon mustard
⅓	lime juice
½	cup olive oil
6	pork tenderloin steaks

COMBINE 1st 5 ingredients in a bowl.
PLACE marinade & pork in a large sealable plastic bag.
SEAL bag. **PRESS** out excess air.
PLACE in refrigerator.
MARINATE for 2 hours.
BASTE with marinade occasionally.
GRILL until desired doneness.

Q: What do you call a smart blonde?
A: A golden retriever.

Salsa Pork Steaks
"Any Blonde Can Salsa"

1	envelope dry taco seasoning
1	teaspoon pepper
1	pound boneless pork, $3/4$ inch cubes
1	teaspoon oil
1	cup chunky salsa
$1/3$	cup peach preserves

RUB pork with 1st 2 ingredients.
HEAT oil on medium-high heat in a large skillet.
BROWN pork all over for 5 minutes.
STIR occasionally. **ADD** remaining ingredients.
REDUCE heat to low. **COVER**. **SIMMER**.

Q: What do you call a basement full of blondes?
A: A whine cellar.

Artichoke Bacon Frittata
"Lisa Lent Me Ham"

1	onion, chopped
2	Tablespoons margarine
2	(6 ounce) jars marinated artichoke hearts, reserve liquid from 1 jar
8	eggs, beaten
1/2	cup grated Parmesan cheese
1/3	cup bread crumbs
6	bacon slices, cooked, crumbled
1	cup shredded Monterey Jack cheese

SAUTÉ 1st 2 ingredients in a large skillet.
ADD artichokes & reserved liquid.
HEAT 2 minutes.
COMBINE mixture with next 4 ingredients.
POUR in a pam-sprayed 9x9 baking dish.
BAKE at 325 degrees for 1 hour & 25 minutes.
SPRINKLE with cheese. **BAKE** 5 more minutes.

Q: What does a blonde make best for dinner?
A: Reservations.

---

www.anotherblondemoment.com

Asparagus Bacon Pie
"Oh Spare Us! the Fat"

2	cups shredded cheddar cheese
1	(8 ounce) can mushrooms, drained
1	frozen deep dish pie crust
1	(16 ounce) can asparagus
5	bacon slices, cooked, crumbled
1	cup milk
6	eggs, beaten
1/2	teaspoon Italian seasoning
1/8	teaspoon pepper

SPRINKLE 1st 2 ingredients in bottom of crust.
ARRANGE asparagus in crust in a wheel.
COMBINE remaining ingredients in a bowl.
POUR over asparagus.
BAKE at 350 degrees for 35 minutes.

Q: How many blondes does it take to make a circuit?
A: Two, One to stand in the bathtub, and another to pass her the blow dryer!

---

www.anotherblondemoment.com

Broccoli Ham Bake
"Wendy Hammed it Up"

2	cups ham, cooked, chopped
1	(4 ounce) can mushrooms, drained
½	teaspoon salt
3	drops hot sauce
2	cups shredded Monterey Jack cheese
1	(16 ounce) frozen chopped broccoli
1½	cups bisquick
3	cups milk
6	eggs, beaten

COMBINE all ingredients in a large bowl.
POUR in pam-sprayed 2-quart casserole dish.
BAKE at 350 degrees for 1 hour.

Fettuccine Ham
"Mama Anne Got Hammed"

1	Tablespoon margarine
3	cups ham, cooked, diced
2	cups heavy cream
1	cup grated Parmesan cheese
1	teaspoon salt
1	(16 ounce) fettuccine, cooked according to directions

MELT margarine in a large pot.
STIR in remaining ingredients.
SIMMER for 20 minutes.
STIR occasionally. **SERVE.**

www.anotherblondemoment.com

Monterey Jack Ham Bake
"Is that a Fact?"

½	stick margarine, melted
1	loaf of bread, each slice cut in half
3	cups shredded Monterey Jack cheese
3	(4 ounce) cans chopped green chilies
3	cups ham, cooked, chopped
4	eggs, beaten
2	cups milk
½	teaspoon salt

POUR margarine in 9x13 baking dish.
PLACE bread slices over margarine.
LAYER ½ cheese, chilies and ham.
REPEAT.
COMBINE last 3 ingredients.
POUR over ham and cheese mixture.
PUT in refrigerator overnight.
BAKE at 350 degrees for 50-60 minutes.

Q: Why do blondes like lightning?
A: They think someone is taking their picture.

---

www.anotherblondemoment.com

Tortellini Ham
"A Twisted Piece"

1	Tablespoon margarine, melted
2	cups ham, cooked, chopped
1	(10 ounce) frozen green peas
1	(8 ounce) fresh sliced mushrooms
1	(16 ounce) jar Alfredo pasta sauce
2	(8 ounce) tortellini (refrigerated section), cooked according to directions

COMBINE all ingredients in a large pot.
SIMMER for 30 minutes.
STIR occasionally. **SERVE.**

Hash Brown Crock-Pot
"Shred Some Butchy"

1	pound frozen hash brown potatoes
1	cup buttermilk
1	jar Cheez-Whiz
1	can cream of mushroom soup
2	cups ham, chopped
½	onion, chopped

COMBINE all ingredients in a crock-pot.
COOK on **MEDIUM** for 4 hours.

www.anotherblondemoment.com

Hash Brown Cheesey
"Got Brown or Blonde"

2	cups frozen hash brown potatoes
1	cup shredded Monterey Jack cheese/jalapeño peppers
1	cup ham, cooked, chopped
1	cup shredded Swiss cheese
2	eggs, beaten
½	cup half-n-half cream

PLACE potatoes in pam-sprayed 9x13 dish.
BAKE at 400 degrees for 20 minutes.
REMOVE from oven. **LET** stand 10 minutes.
LAYER next 3 ingredients in order given.
COMBINE last 2 ingredients in a bowl. **MIX** well.
POUR over cheese.
BAKE at 350 degrees for 25 minutes.

Q: Why are blondes hurt by people's words?
A: Because people keep hitting them with dictionaries.

---

www.anotherblondemoment.com

Rice Ham Pie
"A Pine Cone in Jaxon"

1	pie crust (in refrigerated section)
2	cups ham, cooked, chopped
1	(6 ounce) box long grain wild rice, cooked
1	(4 ounce) can sliced mushrooms, drained
3	eggs, beaten
1	cup sour cream
1	Tablespoon Dijon mustard
½	teaspoon salt
2	cups shredded Swiss cheese, divided

BAKE crust at 425 degrees for 10-12 minutes.
COMBINE next 3 ingredients in a bowl.
COMBINE next 3 ingredients in a separate bowl.
SPRINKLE 1 cup cheese on bottom of crust.
SPREAD ham mixture over cheese.
POUR egg mixture over ham mixture.
BAKE at 375 degrees for 30 minutes.
SPRINKLE with remaining cheese.
PLACE in oven until cheese melts.

www.anotherblondemoment.com

Black Bean Salsa & Pork
"Any Brunette Can Salsa"

2	teaspoons chili powder
1/2	teaspoon salt
1/2	teaspoon pepper
2	Tablespoons oil
2	pound boneless pork tenderloin, sliced thin

COMBINE 1st 3 ingredients in a bowl.
RUB chili powder mixture on pork.
POUR oil in a large skillet.
BROWN pork for 15 minutes on each side.

BLACK BEAN SALSA:

1	(15 ounce) can black beans, rinsed
1	(24 ounce) carton refrigerated citrus fruit, drained
1	ripe avocado, sliced
2/3	cup Italian dressing

COMBINE all salsa ingredients in a large bowl.
SERVE over pork.

Black Bean Mexican Pork
"Pork His Beany Weenie"

2	pound boneless pork tenderloin, cut into 1-inch cubes
3	Tablespoons oil
1	(15 ounce) can black beans, rinsed
1	can fiesta nacho cheese soup
1	(15 ounce) can stewed tomatoes
1	cup instant brown rice, cooked
¾	cup salsa
2	teaspoons ground cumin
1	cup shredded Mexican 3-cheese blend

BROWN 1st 2 ingredients in a large pot. **DRAIN.**
ADD next 6 ingredients to pork.
COOK on medium heat until bubbly.
STIR occasionally.
SPOON in a pam-sprayed 2-quart casserole.
BAKE at 350 degrees for 30-40 minutes.
REMOVE dish from oven.
SPRINKLE with cheese.

How to 'DESERT' a Mate

RECIPES for 'BREAKING UP FOR GOOD'

'MERRY GO ROUND PIE'

1	teaspoon of reality
0	procrastination
1	organized meeting
1	cup of negative moments
1	cup of positive moments
2	cups of forgiveness
0	loneliness

PREPARE the well-considered desire to break-up.
POUR out procrastination which is a thief of time.
DON'T be a 'miserable cowart' by sending a text or an email. **SET** up a meeting.
ADD the negative moments.
STIR in the positive moments.
ADD both cups of forgiveness.
DON'T save the relationship in fear of being lonely.

YIELD: NO LOOKING BACK!

My boyfriend and I broke up over religious differences. He thought he was God, and I didn't.

---

www.anotherblondemoment.com

RECIPES for 'BREAKING UP FOR GOOD'

'YO-YO CAKE'

0   communication
0   intimacy
5   friends
7   gallons of activities

COMBINE 1st 2 ingredients.
POUR in friends to go shopping or talking.
ADD tennis, golfing, biking, running, fishing, reading, and praying to your activities.
MOVE on when you are ready.

A blonde suspects that her boyfriend is cheating on her, so she goes out and buys a gun. She goes to his apartment with the gun in hand. Sure enough, when she opens the door, she finds her boyfriend in the arms of a redhead. She points the gun at her boyfriend and stares him down for a moment. Suddenly, she's overcome with grief, so she puts the gun up to the side her head. Her boyfriend screams, "Honey, don't do it..." The blonde yells back, "Shut up! You're next!"

www.anotherblondemoment.com

Dessert Recipes
(Bars, Cakes, Cookies, Pies)

How to 'DESERT' a Mate
(RECIPES for 'BREAKING UP FOR GOOD')

www.anotherblondemoment.com

Dessert Recipes
(Bars, Cakes, Cookies, Pies)

Q: Why do blondes have see-through lunch box lids?
A: So they will know if it is morning or afternoon.

---

www.anotherblondemoment.com

Butterfinger Bars
"Tootie Green's Buttered Fingers"

1	cup all-purpose flour
1/4	cup brown sugar
1/2	cup margarine, melted
1	(8 ounce) cream cheese, softened
1	cup powdered sugar
1	cup Cool Whip, thawed
2	cups milk
2	small boxes instant vanilla pudding
4	Butterfinger candy bars, crumbled

COMBINE 1st 3 ingredients in a bowl.
PAT in a pam-sprayed 9x13 baking dish.
BAKE at 350 degrees for 15 to 20 minutes.
CREAM next 3 ingredients in a bowl.
SPOON on top of crust.
COMBINE next 2 ingredients in a bowl.
SPOON over cream cheese mixture.
SPRINKLE butterfingers over pudding mixture.
REFRIGERATE. CUT into squares.

Chip Squares
"A Palace Drug Square"

1	(8 ounce) can crescent rolls
1	cup white vanilla chips
1	cup chocolate chips
1	cup slivered almonds
1	cup cashews, chopped
1	can sweetened condensed milk

PRESS rolls in bottom and ½ inch up sides of pam-sprayed 9x13 baking dish.

BAKE at 375 degrees for 5 minutes.

LAYER next 4 ingredients over cooked dough, in order given.

POUR condensed milk over top.

RETURN to oven. **BAKE** 20-25 more minutes.

COOL for 1 hour. **CUT** into squares.

Q: Why do blondes hate M&M's?
A: They're too hard to peel.

---

www.anotherblondemoment.com

Oreo Bars
"Lay Her This Ol' House"

1	(20 ounce) package oreo cookies, crushed
1/2	cup margarine, melted
1	(8 ounce) cream cheese, softened
1	(12 ounce) Cool Whip, divided in half
1/4	cup powdered sugar
1	large instant chocolate pudding, follow directions

COMBINE 1st 2 ingredients in a bowl.
PLACE on bottom of 9x13 baking dish.
REFRIGERATE for 30 minutes.
CREAM next 3 ingredients in a bowl.
SPOON on top of oreos.
REFRIGERATE for 30 minutes.
SPOON pudding on top of cream cheese mixture.
REFRIGERATE for 30 minutes.
TOP with other half of Cool Whip.
CUT into squares.

www.anotherblondemoment.com

Pecan Pie Bars
"A Borders Bar"

1	box yellow cake mix
1	stick margarine, melted
4	eggs, divided 1 egg, 3 eggs, beaten
1½	cups corn syrup
½	cup brown sugar
2	cups pecans, chopped

MIX cake mix, margarine & 1 egg in a large bowl.
MEASURE out ⅔ cup of batter & **SET** aside.
SPREAD remaining batter in bottom of pam-sprayed 9x13 baking dish.
BAKE at 325 degrees for 15 minutes. **COOL**.
MIX reserved batter & remaining ingredients.
POUR pecan mixture over baked cake mix.
BAKE at 325 degrees for 40 minutes. **COOL**.
CUT into bars.

A government study has shown that blondes do have more fun. They just don't remember who with.

www.anotherblondemoment.com

Sweet Potato Bars
"A Mission Inn the Hills"

1	box yellow cake mix, reserved 1 cup
1/2	cup margarine, melted
3	eggs, divided 1 egg, 2 eggs, beaten
3	cups sweet potatoes, mashed **OR**
	2 (15 ounce) cans sweet potatoes, mashed
2/3	cup milk
1/2	cup brown sugar
1	Tablespoon pumpkin pie spice
6	Tablespoons margarine
1	cup pecans, chopped
1/4	cup sugar

COMBINE 1st 2 ingredients and 1 egg in a bowl.
SPREAD in a pam-sprayed 9x13 baking dish.
WHISK 2 eggs and next 4 ingredients.
POUR over cake mix batter.
CUT margarine & last 2 ingredients in reserved cake mix.
POUR over sweet potato mixture.
BAKE at 350 degrees for 1 hour.
COOL for 10 minutes. **CUT** into squares.

www.anotherblondemoment.com

Banana Split Cake
"Krazy Larry Split"

1	box yellow cake mix
½	cup brown sugar
3	teaspoons cinnamon
1	cup water
½	cup oil
2	ripe bananas, mashed
3	eggs, beaten

COMBINE all ingredients in a bowl. **MIX** well.
POUR in a pam-sprayed 9x13 baking dish.
BAKE at 350 degrees for 40-45 minutes.

Blueberry Cake
"Chateau Elan Berried"

1	box yellow cake mix
1	(8 ounce) cream cheese, softened
½	cup oil
3	eggs, beaten
1	(15 ounce) can blueberries, drained
2	teaspoons vanilla

MIX all ingredients in a large bowl.
POUR in a pam-sprayed bundt pan.
BAKE at 350 degrees for 50 minutes.

www.anotherblondemoment.com

Butterfinger Chocolate Cake
"A Sweet Impression"

1	box Devil's Food cake mix
1⅓	cups water
½	cup oil
3	eggs, beaten
1	(8 ounce) jar caramel topping
1	(14 ounce) can condensed milk
4	(2 ounce) butterfinger candy bars
1	(12 ounce) Cool Whip, thawed
1	(8 ounce) cream cheese, softened

BEAT 1st 4 ingredients in a bowl with a mixer.
POUR batter in a pam-sprayed 9x13 baking dish.
BAKE at 350 degrees for 50 minutes.
POKE holes with a straw in warm cake.
MIX last 5 ingredients in a bowl.
SPREAD over cake. **REFRIGERATE.**

Q: Why do men like blonde jokes?
A: Because they can understand them.

---

www.anotherblondemoment.com

Cinnamon Sugar Cake
"Flaunted Blonde"

1	box yellow cake mix
¾	cup oil
1	cup sour cream
½	cup sugar
4	eggs, beaten

COMBINE 1st 5 ingredients in a bowl.
POUR ½ cake batter in pam-sprayed bundt pan.

CINNAMON SUGAR:

½	teaspoon cinnamon
3	Tablespoons sugar

MIX cinnamon-sugar mixture in a small bowl.
SPRINKLE ½ cinnamon sugar over batter.
ADD remaining batter.
SPRINKLE with remaining cinnamon-sugar.
BAKE at 350 degrees for 1 hour.

Q: How do you get a one-armed blonde out of a tree?
A: Wave to her.

---

www.anotherblondemoment.com

Cranberry Bundt Cake
"A Queen's Garden"

1	box lemon cake mix
1	(3 ounce) cream cheese, softened
3/4	cup milk
4	eggs, beaten
1 1/2	cup frozen cranberries, chopped
1/4	cup sugar

BEAT 1st 4 ingredients with a mixer.
BEAT for 2 minutes until smooth.
FOLD last 2 ingredients into batter.
POUR in a pam-sprayed bundt pan.
BAKE at 350 degrees for 1 hour.

I told my blonde girlfriend that I was going skeet shooting.

She told me she didn't know how to cook them.

www.anotherblondemoment.com

Key Lime Cake
"Tara that Point"

1	box lemon cake mix
1	small box lemon instant pudding
1	cup water
1	cup oil
4	eggs, beaten
4	teaspoons key lime juice

BEAT all ingredients in a bowl with a mixer.
POUR in a pam-sprayed 9x13 baking dish.
BAKE at 325 degrees for 55-60 minutes.
PRICK top of cake with fork while still warm.

GLAZE:
2	cups powdered sugar
1/3	cup key lime juice

MIX glaze ingredients in a bowl.
POUR over warm cake.

Orange Cake
"Orange You Gabing & Dabing?"

1	box orange cake mix
1	small instant vanilla pudding
4	eggs, beaten
$\frac{1}{2}$	cup oil
$\frac{3}{4}$	cup orange juice, divided $\frac{1}{2}$ cup, $\frac{1}{4}$ cup
1	cup powdered sugar

COMBINE 1st 5 ingredients in a bowl.
POUR in a pam-sprayed bundt pan.
BAKE at 350 degrees for 40-45 minutes.
COOL for 15 minutes.
MIX $\frac{1}{4}$ cup orange juice & sugar.
POUR over warm cake.

A blonde's response to the comment, "THINK about it!"
"I don't have to think — I'm blonde!"

Chocolate Cookies
"A Georgia Chocolate Moose"

2	**boxes chocolate cake mix**
1	**box brownie mix**
3	**eggs, beaten**
1	**cup oil**
2	**cups water**
1	**teaspoon vanilla**

MIX all ingredients in a large bowl.
SPOON on a pam-sprayed cookie sheet.
BAKE at 325 degrees for 8-10 minutes.
MAKES 6 dozen. Batter freezes well.

Cream Cheese Cookies
"For Friends in Lexington"

1	**(8 ounce) cream cheese, softened**
1/4	**cup margarine, melted**
1/4	**teaspoon vanilla**
1	**egg white**
1	**cup pecans, chopped**
1	**box yellow cake mix**

BLEND 1st 5 ingredients in a bowl.
ADD 1/3 cup of cake mix at a time.
MIX well. **CHILL** dough for 30 minutes.
SPOON on pam-sprayed cookie sheet.
BAKE at 375 degrees for 8-10 minutes.

www.anotherblondemoment.com

Oatmeal Cookies
"Are You an Early Settler?"

1	cup self-rising flour
1	cup quick oats
½	cup sugar
2	egg whites
⅓	cup corn syrup
1	teaspoon vanilla

MIX 1st 3 ingredients in a bowl. **STIR** well.
ADD remaining 3 ingredients. **MIX** well.
SPOON on pam-sprayed cookie sheet.
BAKE at 375 degrees for 8-10 minutes.

White Chocolate Cookies
"A Fair Hope Picture Show"

1	box white cake mix
½	cup oil
1	cup white chocolate chips
2	eggs, beaten
2	Tablespoons water
1	teaspoon vanilla

COMBINE all ingredients in a bowl. **MIX** well.
SPOON on a pam-sprayed cookie sheet.
BAKE at 350 degrees for 10-15 minutes.

www.anotherblondemoment.com

Apple Pie
"The Apple of Your Eye"

4	apples, finely chopped
1	cup sugar divided ³⁄₄ cup, ¹⁄₄ cup
1¹⁄₂	cups sour cream
2	eggs, beaten
¹⁄₂	teaspoon vanilla
1	9 inch deep-dish pie shell
¹⁄₄	cup margarine, melted
¹⁄₃	cup flour
1	teaspoon cinnamon

MIX 1st 5 ingredients in a bowl.
POUR in pie shell.
BAKE at 450 degrees for 30 minutes.
COMBINE ¹⁄₄ cup sugar & remaining
3 ingredients.
POUR over pie.
REDUCE temperature to 325 degrees.
BAKE for 20 more minutes.

Q: Why do blondes work seven days a week?
A: So you don't have to retrain them on Monday.

---

www.anotherblondemoment.com

Butterscotch Pecan Pie
"Arnett Buttered that Ring"

1	(12 ounce) bag butterscotch chips
1	cup corn syrup
4	eggs, beaten
½	teaspoon salt
1	cup pecans, chopped
1	9-inch pie shell, unbaked

MELT chips in microwave until creamy.
COMBINE 1st 5 ingredients in a bowl.
POUR mixture in pie shell.
BAKE at 350 degrees for 50 minutes.

Coconut Macaroon Pie
"This 'N That Nut"

1½	cups coconut flakes
1½	cup sugar
½	cup pecans, chopped
2	eggs, beaten
½	cup margarine, melted
	Pinch of salt
½	cup water
¼	cup flour
1	9-inch pie shell, unbaked

COMBINE 1st 8 ingredients in a bowl.
POUR mixture in pie shell.
BAKE at 325 degrees for 45 minutes.
LET stand for 45 minutes before serving.

www.anotherblondemoment.com

Lemon Cherry Pie
"A Mississippi Gift"

1	9-inch deep-dish graham cracker crust
1	(21 ounce) cherry pie filling
1	(8 ounce) Cool Whip, thawed, divided ½
1	(8 ounce) cream cheese, softened
1	cup milk
1	small lemon instant pudding mix

SPREAD ½ the pie filling in pie crust.
COMBINE remaining 4 ingredients in a bowl.
SPREAD over pie filling.
SPREAD ½ Cool Whip over cream cheese mixture.
SPOON remaining pie filling over Cool Whip.
REFRIGERATE at least 3 hours.

White Chocolate Raspberry Pie
"Oddlee Unik Pie"

2	cups fresh raspberries
1	graham cracker pie crust
1½	cups milk
2	small white chocolate instant pudding
1	(8 ounce) Cool Whip, thawed
¾	teaspoon lemon peel, grated

PLACE raspberries in bottom of pie crust.
COMBINE remaining ingredients in a bowl.
POUR pudding mixture over raspberries.
REFRIGERATE for 4 hours.

www.anotherblondemoment.com

INDEX

INDEX

INDEX

INDEX

INDEX

INDEX